LEGAL EDUCATION IN INDIA

Prof. Chandra Krishnamurthy
Vice Chancellor
SNDT Women's University,
Mumbai.

Himalaya Publishing House
MUMBAI • NEW DELHI • NAGPUR • BENGALURU • HYDERABAD • CHENNAI • PUNE • LUCKNOW • AHMEDABAD • ERNAKULAM • BHUBANESWAR • INDORE • KOLKATA

First Edition : 2009
Second Edition : 2011

Published by	:	Mrs. Meena Pandey for **Himalaya Publishing House Pvt. Ltd.,** "Ramdoot", Dr. Bhalerao Marg, Girgaon, **Mumbai - 400 004.** Phone: 022-23860170/23863863, Fax: 022-23877178 **Email: himpub@vsnl.com; Website: www.himpub.com**
Branch Offices	:	
New Delhi	:	"Pooja Apartments", 4-B, Murari Lal Street, Ansari Road, Darya Ganj, New Delhi - 110 002. Phone: 011-23270392, 23278631; Fax: 011-23256286
Nagpur	:	Kundanlal Chandak Industrial Estate, Ghat Road, Nagpur - 440 018. Phone: 0712-2738731, 3296733; Telefax: 0712-2721215
Bengaluru	:	No. 16/1 (Old 12/1), 1st Floor, Next to Hotel Highlands, Madhava Nagar, Race Course Road, Bengaluru - 560 001. Phone: 080-32919385; Telefax: 080-22286611
Hyderabad	:	No. 3-4-184, Lingampally, Besides Raghavendra Swamy Matham, Kachiguda, Hyderabad - 500 027. Phone: 040-27560041, 27550139; Mobile: 09848130433
Chennai	:	No. 85/50, Bazullah Road, T. Nagar, Chennai - 600 017. Phone: 044-28144004/28144005
Pune	:	First Floor, "Laksha" Apartment, No. 527, Mehunpura, Shaniwarpeth (Near Prabhat Theatre), Pune - 411 030. Phone: 020-24496323/24496333
Lucknow	:	Jai Baba Bhavan, Church Road, Near Manas Complex and Dr. Awasthi Clinic, Aliganj, Lucknow - 226 024. Phone: 0522-2339329, 4068914; Mobile: 09305302158, 09415349385, 09389593752
Ahmedabad	:	114, "SHAIL", 1st Floor, Opp. Madhu Sudan House, C.G. Road, Navrang Pura, Ahmedabad - 380 009. Phone: 079-26560126; Mobile: 09327324149, 09314679413
Ernakulam	:	39/104 A, Lakshmi Apartment, Karikkamuri Cross Rd., Ernakulam, Cochin - 622011, Kerala. Phone: 0484-2378012, 2378016; Mobile: 09344199799
Bhubaneswar	:	5 Station Square, Bhubaneswar - 751 001. (Odisha) Mobile: 09861046007
Indore	:	Kesardeep Avenue Extension, 73, Narayan Bagh, Flat No. 302, IIIrd Floor, Near Humpty Dumpty School, Narayan Bagh, Indore - 452 007 (M.P.). Mobile: 09301386468
Kolkata	:	108/4, Beliaghata Main Road, Near ID Hospital, Opp. SBI Bank, Kolkata - 700 010, Phone: 033-32449649; Mobile: 09910440956
DTP by	:	HPH, Editorial Office, Bhandup (Priya)
Printed by	:	**M/s. Aditya Offset Process (I) Pvt. Ltd., Hyderabad.**

PREFACE

The last century of the last **millennium** was one of the worst in recorded history for war, conflict between men and men, nation and nation and for flagrant violation of human rights. On the other hand, the last century of the last millennium has also generated the promise of improvement and development in the field of science and technology including communication and information technology and law. That century also helped us to arrive at new economic, social, ecological and political arrangements all over the world. New horizons were opened in the fields of trade, commerce, science and technology and law. Various new areas in the field of law were opened. The world is heading towards rapid progress in all fields including law. Globalization has changed dynamism of entire polity and society. Now, the whole world is giving importance upon knowledge economy. Since the development of knowledge economy remains an important goal of the developed and developing countries, the establishment of educational institutions of global excellence along with changed new curriculum of global standard ought to become the priority of the developing country like India. Universities worldwide are preparing them to face the challenges of globalization. Some of the famous Universities of the world like Cambridge, Harvard, New York, Oxford, Stanford and Yale are gearing themselves up to cope with the changing situation of internationalization of education. Globalization and the changing dimension of the Indian economy and polity have thrown up new challenges before us.

It is in this **international** and global spectacle. This is not meant to be a polemical or critical piece but is an earnest appeal to the concerned authorities to do the needful in the changed era of globalization. Today, legal education requires modernization and a complete relook both at the teaching methodology and the curriculum development. It should be a comprehensive capsule to cater to the various stakeholders of the society.

Prof. Chandra Krishnamurthy

INTRODUCTION

The vision of legal education is to provide justice-oriented education essential to the realization of the values enshrined in the Constitution of India. Keeping this vision in mind, legal education must aim to achieve in preparing legal professionals who will be the future leaders playing decisive roles. Legal Education should not only prepare practicing advocates in the court but also as academic, legislators, judges, policy makers, public officials, civil society activists as well as legal counsels in the private sectors. Legal education should also focus on world-class legal education, internationalization where the nature and organization of law and legal practice are undergoing a progressive change. Report of Knowledge Commission (2008) speaks about multifaceted approach that should be adopted.

A lawyer should display his abilities for argumentation, debates, discussion and the spirit of accommodation. A lawyer must also possess a rare combination of team spirit and leadership. He should know how to get co-operation. He should be visionary and team builder. Acquisitions of these abilities calls for a reasonably higher level of knowledge not only in law but also in subjects like History, English, Psychology, Sociology, Economics, etc. Thomas Jafferson, the third President of US is reported to have mentioned to the students of Yale University that if one happens to be a law student, there is no area of study which could be excluded from his curriculum.

It remains the open fact that we don't have sufficiently trained teachers for deployment on various law schools. Nor are the available teachers adequately equipped for quality teaching. What are the qualities required by a good teacher? A teacher should be a scholar and willing to work hard. He should acquire the knowledge by reading in each branch of law by reading at higher level. His approach should not be to acquire what is law but what ought to be law. To teach at this level, he should have foundation in the subject and then develop skills for higher thinking and argumentations. He should be in a position to impart the skills of analysis of case laws and the interpretation of statutes. He should be a visionary.

Legal education in modern times is expected to fulfill a range of functions, in addition to educating lawyers and judges. Legal education has to support development including that of the market. It has to provide the citizen, the knowledge required to exercise civic responsibilities and rights. Civil servants and law enforcement officials need understanding of law and its processes.

So do politicians. With growing complexity ir governance, new activities call for specialized kinds of legal education. Of course, all these diverse objects of legal education need not necessarily depend on formal University-based legal education. The law schools are patterned after an inherited model (except perhaps the 5-year integrated LL.B. course after higher secondary school) which has limited outlook, content, methods and organization. To a large extent, they are controlled by legal practitioners and, as such, influenced by private practice-oriented, litigation-based approach to legal studies. The content of law study does not adequately reflect the role of law in development nor tend to engage with social movements for change. The method is not inter-disciplinary and tends to treat as an independent, self-contained discipline unconcerned with consequences or outcomes and divorced from social needs and realities. It neither cares to identify professional skills nor impart training in them. It does not encourage empirical research nor interrogate policy assumptions or impact of laws on behavior. Without any planning and effective regulation, the system of legal education produces "half-baked" law graduates is intended. Above all, ethics is no where taught or learnt in the market of a lawyer under the existing system.

The Five-year Integrated LL.B. course and the National Law School movement did make a change, though small, in the way law education is imparted in the country. However, compared to the large number of persons graduating every year through the conventional steam (part-time, postgraduate three-year LL.B. course), the number coming from National Law Schools and similar institutions are too small to make a difference. Moreover, those graduating from these elite law schools are almost entirely absorbed by the private corporate sector thereby leaving the district bar and the subordinate judiciary not being able to get the services of better trained professionals.

BRIEF CONTENTS

1

Legal Education and The Advocates Act, 1961

INTRODUCTION

The provisions of Sec. 7(1)(h) of the Advocates Act, 1961 enable the Bar Council of India to lay down the standards of legal education required for students who seek enrolment to the Bar. It is therefore necessary to refer to some aspects of the standards, particularly those relating to legal skills. The minimum standards of legal education has been laid down by the Bar Council of India.

Several efforts have been made from time to time, to improve standards of legal education. The following reports are to be understood to redevelop the legal education. (1) The 14th Report of the Law Commission headed by Sri M.C. Setalvad is one of the best and elaborate reports on Legal education. It is something which every person must read and (2) The UGC Curriculum Reports 1988-90 and 2001 should also be taken into consideration. Eminent professors, including Prof. Upendra Baxi were the contributors. One must also read (3) Ahmadi Committee Report which contains extracts of letters of the Chairman, Bar Council of India and Chairman, University-Grants Commission, and views of Chief Justices of various High Courts in the matter of Legal education and various suggestions which were given regarding the courses of study, attendance, entrance examination, final examination, the lecture method, case method, problem method, constitution of Committees and membership, and need for apprenticeship and Bar examination. In this Chapter, we are referring briefly to some of these aspects and we propose to lay emphasis on Legal Skills and Values as enunciated in the Mac Crate Report of USA.

Standards of Legal Education and Legal Skills:

In the Bar Council of India rules, Part IV (as amended upto 30.11.1998) dealing with the subject of 'Standards of Legal Education and Recognition of Degrees in Law for Admission as Advocates', Section A refers to 5-year law course after 10+2 or 11+1, Section B relates to 3-year law course after graduation, and Section C refers to Rules regarding inspection of law colleges by State Bar Councils. Again Schedule I contains a list of the Directives issued under Rule 21 in Section A or under Rule 14 in Section B. Schedule II is the questionnaire to be answered by any college which is seeking affiliation. Schedule III deals with Proforma for Inspection of law colleges and Schedule IV with the Form of Annual Return to be submitted by the law colleges. We also have the Training Rules, 1995 made under sec. 24(3)(d) of the Advocates Act, 1961 which have been struck down by the Supreme court as being *ultra vires* of the Act or rather beyond the rule-making power.

Recently, new Proforma formats have been prescribed for application seeking permission to open law colleges and in respect of inspections, compliance, responses in respect to standards of legal education, recognition of degrees, etc.

The Ahmadi Committee Report dealt elaborately with the methods of teaching. It referred to the "case method" introduced by Prof. Langdell of Harvard University and to the "problem method" pioneered by Prof. Carl Llewellyn and Judge Jerome Frank and the Notre Dame Law School. The Report referred to Rule 21 of the Rules and to Schedule I dealing with the 5-year course which contains the following directive:

"10. Every university shall endeavour to supplement the lecture method with the case method, tutorials and other modern techniques of imparting legal education."

The Report recommended as follows:

"This Rule must be amended in a mandatory form and we should include problem method, moot courts, mock trials and other aspects in this Rule and make them compulsory."

In tune with the above recommendations, we find in the 5-year course syllabus that Rule 2(c) says as follows:

"2(c): That the course of study in law has been by regular attendance for the requisite number of **lectures, tutorials, moot courts** and **practical training** given by a college...."

Rule 3(2) refers to contact and correspondence programme, tutorials, home assignments, library, clinical work etc. — in all 30 hours per week but classroom lectures should not be less than 20 hours.

Rule 9(1) lists 6 subjects for part I (compulsory). Rule 9(2) lists 21 subjects for part II (compulsory). Rule 9(3) lists 15 subjects (optional) out of which three have to be selected. Rule 9(4) refers to 6 months practical training which will include the following compulsory papers:

Paper I: Moot court, pre-trial preparations and participation in trial proceedings — 10 marks for each, total 30 marks. Observance of trial in two cases, one civil and one criminal case (30 marks).

Interviewing techniques and pre-trial preparations (30 marks). Viva-voice (10 marks).

Paper II: Drafting, pleading (15 exercises) and conveyancing (15 exercises).

Civil, criminal, writ petition and drafting sale deed, mortgage etc.

Paper III: Professional ethics, accountancy for lawyers and Bar-Bench relations — 80 marks. Viva-voice 20 marks.

Paper IV: Deals with public interest lawyers, legal aid and para-legal services (100 marks).

Professional Skills and Professional Values – The Mac Crate Report:

On legal skills, reference to the Mac Crate Report of USA (1992) which is the Report of the 'Task Force on Law Schools and the Profession: Narrowing the Gap", prepared by the American Bar Association. This was followed by subsequent resolution of the ABA House of Delegates in Feb, 1994 and the Report on Learning Professionalism 1996 (Chicago). It is also necessary to refer to the study made by the Law Society of England and Wales on 'Preparatory Skills: Review of the Institute of Professional Studies' (Auckland) 1990; the earlier Reports, namely, Crampton Report on Lawyer Competency (US) (1979) and the Carrrington Report on Training for Public Professions of the Law (1971), Washington. The National Law School, Bangalore is said to have prepared a new curriculum in 2001 based on the Mac Crate and Harvard curriculum, with modifications suited for Indian conditions.

There are 10 chapters in the Mac Crate Report in Parts I to III. Chapter 5 of the Report refers to the 'Statement of Fundamental **Lawyers Skills** and **Professional Values**'. Chapter 7 refers to 'Professional Development during Law School', Chapter 8 to 'Transition from Law Student to Practitioner', Chapter 9 to 'Professional Development after Law School', Chapter 10 refers to the 'Need for a National Institute to Enhance the Process of Professional Development'.

Under Chapter V(A) thereof, the legal skills referred are: (1) legal research, (2) factual investigation, (3) communication, (4) counseling, (5) negotiation, (6) skills required to employ or to advise a client about the options of litigation and alternative dispute resolution mechanisms, (7) the skill to identify the administrative skills necessary to organize and manage legal work effectively and (8) finally, the skill of analyzing the skills involved in recognizing and resolving ethical dilemmas.

Professional values, according to the Mac Crate Report, include 'training in professional responsibilities' and involve more than 'just the specifics of the Code of Professional Responsibility and the Model Rules of Professional Conduct'; they should encompass 'the values of the profession', including the 'obligations and accountability of a professional dealing with the lives and affairs of clients. These values are many, such as, (1) the value of competent representation, analyzing the ideals to which a lawyer should be committed as a member of a profession dedicated to the service of clients, (2) the value of striving to promote justice, fairness and morality; the ideals to which a lawyer should be committed as a member of a profession that bears special responsibilities for the quality of justice, (3) the value of striving to improve the profession; explore the ideals to which a lawyer should be committed as a member of a 'self-governing' profession, (4) the value of professional self-development, analyzing the ideals to which the lawyer should be committed as a member of a 'learned profession'. The Report also refers to the relationship between the 'skills' and the 'values'.

Chapter V(b) of the Report refers to 'Fundamental lawyers skills' as follows:

(1) diagnosing a problem, generating alternative solutions and strategies, developing a plan of action, implementing the plan and keeping the planning process open to new information and new ideas.

(2) identifying and formulating legal issues, formulating relevant legal theory, elaborating legal theory, evaluating legal theory and criticising and synthesizing legal argumentation.

(3) knowledge of the nature of Legal Rules and Institutions, knowledge of and ability to use the most fundamental tools of legal research, understanding of the process of devising and implementing a coherent and effective research design.

(4) determining the need for factual investigation, planning a factual investigation, implementing the investigative strategy, memorizing and organizing information in an accessible form, deciding whether to conclude the process of fact gathering, evaluating the information

that has been gathered, assessing the perspective of the recipient of the communication; using effective methods of communication.

(5) Establishing a counselling relationship that respects the nature and bounds of a lawyer's role; gathering information relevant to the decision to be made; analyzing the decision to be made; counseling the client about the decision to be made, ascertaining and implementing the client's decision.

(6) preparing for negotiation, conducting a negotiating session, counseling the client about the terms obtained from the other side in the negotiation and implementing the client's decision.

(7) advise the clients about the options of litigation and alternative dispute resolution, and have a fundamental knowledge of:

 (a) litigation at the trial-court level

 (b) litigation at the appellate level

 (c) advocacy in disputes between and Executive Forms

 (d) proceedings in other Dispute Resolution Forums

(8) skills of efficient management such as formulating goals and principles, developing systems and procedures to ensure that time, effort and resources are allocated efficiently; develop system to ensure work is completed at the appropriate time; develop system or procedures to work effectively with other people, develop system and procedures for efficiently administering the law office.

(9) keep familiar with nature and sources of ethical standards, the means by which ethical standards are enforced, the processes for recognizing and resolving ethical dilemmas.

The Mac Crate Report says that law schools and the practicing bar should look upon the development of lawyers as a **common enterprise.** recognizing that **legal education** and **practicing lawyers** have different capacities and opportunities to impart to future lawyers the skills and values required for the competent and responsible practice of law. Each law school, the Report says, should determine how its school can best help its students to **begin** the process of acquiring the **skills** and **values** that are important in the practice of law. Law schools should be encouraged to develop or expand instruction in such areas as 'problem solving', 'fact investigation', 'communication', 'counselling', 'negotiation', and 'mitigation'.

One has to read the elaborate article by Prof. John J. Costonis, Dean of Vandebilt University: "The Mac Crate Report: Of Loaves, Fishes and the Future of American Education) in vol. 43 (1993), *Journal of Legal Education,*

p. 157, further refers to several important developments in the field of Legal education.

The Bar Council and UGC Committees must also look into similar Reports in UK, Canada and Australia so that our standards match with standards elsewhere and we are able to produce, in all our 460 and odd law schools and the 102 universities which offer legal education, students of the same caliber and knowledge. Apart from that, in the context of liberalization, privatization and globalization, in order to keep pace with international standards and the emergence of new economy — **globalization, privatization and deregulation** have thrown up new challenges. There are today revolutionary changes in information, communication and transportation technologies which require corresponding changes in the legal system. Now, we have introduced many specialized areas of law like intellectual property, corporate law, cyber law, human rights, alternative dispute resolution, international business transactions, in all our law schools. The opening of trade and capital markets as a result of globalization and the retreat of the State from traditional roles have raised new legal issues concerning ways in which poor and marginalized sections can protect themselves from further impoverishment. Special emphasis has to be made on criminal justice. The very nature of law, legal institutions and law practice are in the midst of paradigm shifts.

Legal education must seek to serve distinct interdisciplinary knowledge domains — law and society; law, science and technology; law, economics, commerce and management.

Teaching must focus on building up in the student, skills of analysis, language, drafting and argument. Teachers must bear in mind that while most of the students may choose a professional career as a lawyer, some others may choose a judicial career or career as a legal consultant or law officer in government or an academic career.

Alternative Dispute Resolution systems — mediation, conciliation, arbitration, etc. must be and remain as a compulsory subject.

The curriculum should not make the mandatory element too large but subjects which are in need in the bulk of the courts in the mofussil, in the civil and criminal law, must be mandatory. While subjects mostly in use in the courts at the grass-root level must be mandatory and some new subjects can also be made mandatory, care must be taken to give more choice to the students in the optional subjects.

Syllabus could be structured not merely on the basis of mandatory subjects but also on basis of "credits" as done in the National Law School.

Accreditation and quality assessment of law schools must be introduced by the UGC and BCI to build up a sense of competition between the different law schools. Legal education institutions are not today adequately subject to a rigorous system of quality assessment and accreditation processes. The various well-known parameters for evaluating the performance of a law school must be laid down by the UGC and the BCI and annual rating must be given to each law school and published in the internet to enable prospective students to compete for admission to the best law schools.

If necessary, this task may be performed by the UGC and BCI by taking the help of professional agencies who are well versed in accreditation processes of law schools. There must also be transparency about the quality of the assessment.

Hence, the existing clause (h) of subsection (1) of Section 7 which merely refers to "Promotion of Legal Education and Laying Standards in Consultation with the Universities and State Bar Councils" may include the following suggestions.

(a) for clause (h), the following clauses shall be substituted, namely:- "(h) to promote *legal education* and lay down standards of such education in accordance with the recommendations of the Bar Council Legal Education Committee arrived at in the manner specified in Section 10AA including, in the matter of—

(i) the prescription of standards relating to curriculum, admission of students, appointment and qualification of teachers;

(ii) the appointment of adjunct teachers from the Bar and from among the retired judges;

(iii) the prescription of conditions of service of the law teachers;

(iv) the prescription of student-teacher ratio;

(v) the laying down of guidelines for adopting different leaching methods;

(vi) specifying the conditions as to the location of law colleges, infrastructure, library and management;

(vii) promoting excellence in legal education for the purposes of the accreditation scheme if any, introduced by NAAC;

(viii) promoting alternative dispute resolution as a subject of academic study in the law schools for students;

(ix) promoting continuing education on alternative dispute resolution for legal practitioners.

2

Legal Education to Meet Challenges of Globalization

"Our colleges of law do not hold a place of high esteem either at home or abroad nor has law become an area of profound scholarship and enlightened research."

Dr. Radhakrishnan

INTRODUCTION

Through this chapter, author seeks to address the condition of existing legal education in India including the effectiveness of the existing legal curriculum. This chapter examines the related provisions of GATS and the effects of Globalization upon legal education in India. The author also tries to examine the effectiveness of the recommendations of national knowledge commission, in this context, upon the system of legal education in India. This paper also highlights some suggestions to improve the standard of legal education in the era of Globalization.

LEGAL EDUCATION AND GLOBALIZATION

In a democratic country like India, where rule of law is the driving force of the Government, legal education assumes great significance. *In Keshvanand Bharati vs. State of Kerala,* Hon'ble Supreme court held that rule of law is the basic foundation of our democracy. Rule of law says that "Be you ever so high, the law is above you". Education has wider implication. It stands for development. Education makes men perfect. In the words of Swami Vivekananda, "it is the manifestation of perfection already in man". Again, legal education makes men law-abiding and socially-conscious. Legal education helps in bringing and establishing socio-economic justice. Change is the law of nature and law is the regulator of social change. It is *sine qua non* for the development of rule of law and a sustainable democratic order. In other words, legal education is the heart and the very soul of the society for administering rule of law in a democratic country like ours. Therefore, quality legal education is to be imparted to the people taking into consideration the changing needs of the society and the changing era of globalization. In *Mumbai Vashi vs. State of Maharashtra,* Hon'ble Supreme court held that — "the legal education should be able to meet the ever-growing demands of the society and should be thoroughly equipped to cater to the complexities of different situations."

As per C. Rajkumar, legal education and its importance to establish a rule of law society did not receive any serious priority or attention in the traditional Universities, although due to the **sheer motivation of students themselves** the departments were successful in producing many of the brightest lawyers and some of the best academics in the country. According to him, various law schools in India, however, successfully challenged this institutionalized mediocrity and succeeded in attracting serious students to the study of law. But the lack of researchers in law and absence of due emphasis on research and publications in the existing law schools have led to the absence of an intellectually vibrant environment. The reforms of the higher education system are central to developing a knowledge-based society in India. Within the paradigm of such reforms, drastic steps need to be taken to address the numerous challenges facing legal education in India. Because, law and legal education has an important role to play in protecting rule of law and the democracy as a whole. Lawyers are the backbonee of the society and they are social engineers.

WTO AGREEMENT AND GLOBALIZATION

The World Trade Organization had come into effect from 1st January, 1995 with support of 85 founding member countries including India. India signed the agreement as one of the founder members. The General Agreement on Trade in Services (GATS) of WTO agreement consists of six parts, xxix Articles and 8 Annexure. GATS impose number of general obligations on signatory countries. All signatory countries are bound to abide by the rules of the WTO. GATS require nations to accord "most favoured nation" status. As per this agreement, a member country must provide both market access and "national treatment" to other member countries. As a consequence, we cannot prevent the entry of foreign lawyers into India. If we do so, that will amount to an infringement of the provisions of GATS and WTO. Globalization has brought a tough competition in educational service sectors. We are facing tough competition not only from within but also from outside the country. Internationalization and Globalization of the legal profession and the probable entry of foreign lawyers into India in the near future, poses a serious threat to the legal professionals in India. We have to compete with the knowledge of foreign lawyers. Globalization of the legal profession is likely to introduce a sea change in the entire fabric of law teaching and legal profession in India. The profession of law today to a large extent, requires lawyers to represent clients not only within but also outside national frontiers. After the establishment of WTO and India gets actively involved in trade liberalization, including trade in legal services (under GATS), there is no escape from allowing equal treatment to law persons from other jurisdictions. As a result of the unprecedented changes induced by technology and globalization, all professions including legal profession are forced to rethink their method of management and delivery of services.

Curriculum of Legal Education and Globalization:

The legal education in India is regulated by multiple agencies including University Grants Commission (UGC), Bar Council of India (BCI), The Government and the respective University authorities. For numerous reasons, the quality of legal education in the 1970s was not satisfactory. Several attempts were made to reform curriculum and stricter controls were imposed by the Bar Councils of India at various times but no substantial results were achieved in terms of quality, professionalism and competitiveness in legal education. To come out the problem, the Bar Council of India itself decided to establish a model law school in the private sector or joint sector to bring reform in the legal education. As a result, the National Law School of India University was established in Bangalore in 1986. However, at present, the number of national law schools has increased. At various times, curriculum of legal education was changed by the Bar Council of India. But these were not sufficient to meet the new challenges of globalization in the 21st century.

The National Knowledge Commission (NKC) was, however, established by the Prime Minister of India in 2005 to recommend and undertake reforms in order to make India knowledge-based economy and society. The National Knowledge Commission, while deliberating on issues related to knowledge concepts, recognizes legal education as an important constituent of professional education. The Working Group on legal education, *inter alia,* identified the problems and challenges relating to curriculum and recommended changes and reforms relating to curriculum. The report recommends the development of contemporary curriculum, which is integrated with other disciplines and also ensures regular feedback from stakeholders. The curricula and syllabi must be based in a multidisciplinary body of social science and scientific knowledge. Curriculum development should include expanding the domain of optional courses, providing deeper understanding of professional ethics, modernizing clinic courses, mainstreaming legal aid programmes and developing innovative pedagogic methods. With the advent of globalization, it has become increasingly important to include international and comparative law perspectives. According to C. Rajkumar, in the era of globalization, we should pay attention to four important factors to improve the standard of legal education. These are: Global curriculum, Global faculty, Global degrees and Global interactions. We have to think globally but act locally. Law is one of the most dynamic subjects of the world. Dynamism is the lifeblood of law. A law which is static cannot survive for long and will be rejected by people for whom the law will be implemented. So, to keep pace with the changing situation of the world we have also to change, by addition, subtraction, or cancellation, of the existing curriculum of the legal education in India. Otherwise, in future, it will loosen its importance and will turn into a relic of the past.

Some Suggestions and Conclusion:

The legal education in 21st century should be considered the globalization and its implications on legal held at national and international levels. The Bar Council of India, the State Bar Councils, the State Governments, the University Grants Commission and the Universities have a great role to play for improving the standard of legal education in the country. They should work in a comprehensive manner without any conflict. New avenues should be explored by the Bar Council of India and the University Grants Commission in the era of computer applications and information technology in the legal fields and potential uses of internet in the practice of law and legal education. They should find out the ways and means to meet the new challenges and provide better tools of research and methodology of learning for the generations to come. Bar Council of India, constituted under section 4 of the Advocates Act, 1961, is an apex body for the entire legal profession in India. The Advocates Act, 1961, invests BCI with wide-ranging powers to prescribe standards of legal education for the practice of law. In the opinion of Dr. N.R. Madhava Menon, legal education in India should be liberated from the dominant control of the Bar Councils and entrusted to legal academics with freedom to innovate, experiment and compete globally.

The recommendations of the National Knowledge Commission, in this regard, deserve attention of the Bar, the Judiciary and the Government. The reforms initiated in few law schools all over India have made only a small dent. However, the vision of legal education is to provide justice-oriented education essential to the realization of values mentioned in the Indian Constitution. In keeping with this vision, legal education must aim at preparing legal professionals who will play decisive leadership roles maintaining the highest standards of professional ethics and a spirit of public service. Legal education should also prepare professionals equipped to meet the new challenges and dimensions of internationalization, where the nature and organization of law and legal practice are undergoing a paradigm shift. Existing curriculum should be immediately changed as per recommendation of National Knowledge Commission. Any further delay in this regard will be suicidal. According to Justice A.M. Ahmadi, "We have waited long enough to repair the cracks in the legal education system of this country and it is high time that we rise from armchairs and start the repair work in right earnest".

3

Changing Scenario in Legal Education Future

Legal Education, Liberal and Professional:

Legal education is a small, yet significant component of higher education which is attracting, unlike in the past, a lot of attention today. Legal education, in a liberal sense, involves imparting basic understanding of law, *no* justice systems in order to build a healthy democratic society under rule of law and to promote responsible citizenship with awareness of rights and responsibilities. There is a strong case in this regard to teach the Constitution to all students in schools and colleges. Professional education in law, on the other hand, is concerned with preparation of legally trained persons to act as lawyers and judges for the increasingly numerous tasks of governance, socio-economic reconstruction, adjudication of disputes, conduct of international relations, legal research and reform, etc.

The proposals in respect of liberal education include teaching of appropriate citizenship modules in the School curriculum, introduction of 'law' as a subject in the graduate courses in Colleges and Universities and developing extension programmes in the form of para-legal courses suitable to a wide-range of governmental, para-legal and civil society organizations. Some Universities are already involved in these types of liberal legal education activities which do strengthen rule of law and democratic development particularly at the grass roots. Indira Gandhi Open University's School of Law has embarked on an ambitious agenda for legal education through the distance mode. Teaching of law subjects is also picking up in commerce and management departments, medical and engineering schools and social work institutions, though they are more designed to equip the respective professionals to use legal tools and resources to advance their professional goals, rather than to make an aware citizenry.

What is more important in the immediate future for the country is the quality of professional legal education is still managed by a mix of — good, bad and indifferent institutions. The State of legal education in the country at the time of Independence was neither uniform nor professional, nor standardized to the needs of the young Republic. There were less than fifty colleges teaching law mostly in major cities and that too run on a part-time basis to part-time students not seriously pursuing a career in law. Thus, result was that students who were serious to join the profession and could afford the costs went to England for legal studies. Recognizing the total inadequacy of University education in law, the organized profession in the respective States insisted on compulsory apprenticeship with a senior lawyer for at least an year coupled with a tough Bar Council — conducted examination on professional subjects before anyone could be enrolled for legal practice. Obviously, the situation was unsatisfactory both from the academic and professional points of view. The problem was compounded because of liberal admission to legal practice of people who never went to Universities for legal education but were associated with administration to justice as Vakils, Muktiars, Pleaders and agents for a certain period of time.

When the Indian Advocates Act was enacted by Parliament in 1961, a major change was initiated by entrusting the development and control of legal education to the elected Bar Councils. It was to be organized in consultation with Universities teaching law through a Statutory Committee called the Legal Education Committee. The story of legal education from 1961 till date is a mixed bag of little done, vast undone for which the teachers, students, Bar Councils, Universities Managements and the State/Central Governments have to own up responsibilities. Looking back at these five decades of legal education since 1961, I find a lot of missed opportunities and half-hearted reform efforts resulting in a situation where each step forward was followed by two steps backward in efforts to reform legal education from the morass it has fallen. Perhaps, the challenges of technology and globalization coupled with new opportunities emerging for legally trained persons may now influence the course of professional legal education in better ways of sustained reform for excellence.

The Initial Phase of Expansion and Consolidation

The developments in legal education since 1961 can be grouped in two phases: the first phase was one of expansion and consolidation while the second which is still continuing has been one of quality improvement and increased social relevance.

The concern in the 1960s and 70s has been around unification of standards and consolidation of the new regulatory set-up established under the Bar Council of India. The Advocates Act and Rules framed thereunder envisaged a full-time post-graduate three-year LL.B. course followed by an year-long apprenticeship under a Senior advocate and a Bar Council conducted test as prerequisites for entry to the profession. The curriculum which was made uniform throughout the country contained mostly required courses covering substantive and procedural laws. The teaching method was almost entirely through lectures, sometimes in vernacular language and students depended mainly on guidebooks to pass examinations which where largely memory tests rather than of problem solving and analytical capabilities. The result was absenteeism and proxy in classes, aggressive student politics in campus and widespread copying and fraudulent practices in examinations. The first casually in this turmoil was apprenticeship and Bar-conducted examinations which were dropped by an amendment to the Act enabling everyone with a law degree, however obtained, to enroll as an advocate, non-serious students and disinterested teachers (mostly practicing lawyers) made law education the refuge of students who could not get admitted to other disciplines. The craze for University degrees however led to an uncontrolled expansion to law colleges, mostly run for few hours in the evening by managements who found a source of additional income with little or no investments!

One welcome development during this phase was the enormous growth of law teaching institutions even in small towns and talukas which ensured access to the so-called legal education to everyone who sought it at highly subsidized price. However, an unwelcome consequence of this uncontrolled growth has been the steep decline of already poor standards. The law Curriculum had little relation to professional needs and still less relevance to the problems of democracy and development. The Bar Councils consisting of practicing lawyers have neither the time nor the competence nor the resources to study the problems and respond with corrective measures. The University Grants Commission kept legal education outside its agenda on the ground that it was Bar Council's responsibility.

The Second Phase of Reform for Relevance and Quality

The establishment of the Bar Council of India Trust to support legal education and the repeated demand from a section of the Bar and Bench for better legal education led to a lot of initiatives in the 1980s and 90s, some of which started even during the first phase in some isolated Universities. With assistance from the Ford Foundation, Delhi and Banaras Universities not only evolved an improved curriculum and teaching methods, but also introduced academic exchanges with leading American law schools. A number of young teachers returned with exposure in English and American legal education and experimented innovative measures lo make legal education intellectually stimulating and professionally significant. The Indian Law Institute also lent a helping hand in promoting research activities and textbook production during this period.

The Bar Council of India Trust convened a series of seminars and conferences together with its Legal Education Committee which recommended some structural and institutional reforms. Among these, the most important was the establishment of a model law school to act as a pace-setter in legal education reform. Other recommendations included introduction of an integrated five-year LL.B. (Hons.) programme to replace the existing three-year post-graduate LL.B. course and bringing the apprenticeship scheme back in the enrolment regulations. The University Grants Commission as part of its curriculum development programme appointed a Committee to totally revamp the law curriculum bringing in subjects of contemporary relevance to be taught with an interdisciplinary focus. Under the Academic Staff College scheme of the UGC, a series of faculty development courses were held for law teachers. The LL.M. course was also revised to prepare future teachers with additional skills and knowledge for better discharge of their responsibilities. Several legal periodicals started publication and law publishers not only brought out standard textbooks by Indian scholars but also made Indian reprints of classical legal books available at reasonable prices.

The National Law School Movement, a Turning Point in Legal Education

No development in legal education in post-independent India has made such a decisive and wholesome impact as did the establishment of the National Law School at Bangalore in 1986. There are several features which made a lasting difference in the scheme of things since then. *Firstly,* the induction of students after the 12th standard school education for professional legal studies under the five-year integrated LL.B. (Hons.) course attracted highly talented students to legal education. *Secondly,* law schools got dissociated from the pre-existing pattern of affiliation to conventional Universities and were given independent university status thereby affording a lot of curriculum and pedagogic experimentation and competitive pursuit of excellence. *Thirdly,* the study of social science along with law subjects provided an opportunity to look at legal problems in social context which in turn, enhanced the social relevance of legal education. *Fourthly,* clinical legal education or "learning by doing" received attention of law teachers and students enabling law schools to be increasingly involved in legal aid delivery and community development programmes. And *finally,* impressed by the quality of graduates passing out of the National Law Schools, leading law firms made a beeline to these institutions to recruit them paying handsome salaries not even dreamt by law graduates till then.

Today, fourteen National Law Universities are functioning in as many States established under independent Statutes largely on the model of the Bangalore National Law School. They together offer nearly 1,500 seats every year for which on an average over 15,000 students compete in the Common Law Entrance Test. Along with them, at least another 100 law schools in the Government and private sector impart instruction for the 5-year integrated LL.B. course on the lines of the National Law School curriculum providing opportunities to another 8,000 students or more. There is a healthy competition for academic excellence developing among all these institutions and they are ranked for the benefit of students by media establishments involved in educational surveys. Legal education never had it so good and the present time is easily its golden age. Thanks to the success of the National Law School experiment.

Of course, there are some 400 other law colleges mostly continuing with the traditional scheme under the three-year LL.B. course offering legal education to an estimated 50,000 students! According to one estimate in 2005, there were over 75,500 law students enrolled in nearly 700 colleges or departments of law. On an average, about 50,000 graduates are admitted to the Bar every year in India. Obviously, the National Law School's impact is minimal in the overall scheme of legal education in the country.

Nonetheless, the five-year integrated LL.B. programme with which the National Law School got started, contributed a great deal in revising the legal curriculum and teaching methods in a number of affiliated colleges which could not command the freedom and resources for academic experimentation and innovation. Though the subjects are not being taught in an integrated style, students do get to understand the multiple roles of law in society. Though the skills are not being taught in a professional context, students do find opportunities to learn analytical and problem-solving skills even in the part-time colleges. The popularity of legal aid clinics, moot court competitions and short-term internships in law offices is indicative of the changes that the five-year integrated curriculum has brought about in old-time colleges. A higher degree of seriousness on the part of students and teachers naturally developed compelling the disappearance of many non-serious, degree producing teaching shops which dominated legal education till then.

The net result of changes between 1986 and 2005 initiated by the National Law Schools and the five-year integrated LL.B. programme has seen renewed attention of all concerned, attraction of highly talented students in large numbers to legal education, impressive investment in educational infrastructure, though only in selected institutions and an increasingly competitive market for legally trained persons. The average price of a good law graduate employed by a corporate firm is now over ₹ 30,000 per month and the really outstanding are hired for as high as ₹ 20 lakh a year. Foreign law firms are participating with their Indian counterparts to make campus recruitment of fresh law graduates with some of them getting three or more offers from renowned legal and accounting establishments. In fact, the corporate invasion of National Law Schools has attracted the severest criticism from the judiciary which has been looking forward to the induction of well-trained lawyers in large numbers in the district Bar and the subordinate judiciary from the new institutions.

THE PRESENT SCENARIO: A MIXED BAG

A commentator of the present legal education system obtaining in the country wrote as follows:

"As in many other spheres of activity, in legal education, there are two Indias: the first consists of the 14 national law universities, and probably a similar number of prestigious schools, while the second India comprises the hundreds of law colleges scattered around the country where getting a degree is more important than learning. Waiting for clerical jobs in government, banks and businesses, unemployed youth enroll in those law colleges of the second-rate stream. Every year, the thousand or so graduates of the prestigious schools go on to lucrative jobs in elite law firms while their less smart cousins get by with what they can".

The problem presented today in the legal education front is twofold. *Firstly* to bring in second generation reforms in National Law Schools and similar institutions to allow them to grow to international standards with an agenda which will serve the economic and social development of the country and its unmet legal needs. *Secondly,* it is necessary to bring in broad-based academic and structural reforms to change the character and quality of education in the 600 and odd law colleges which are in varying stages of stagnation and neglect. In fact, the Working Group on Legal Education set-up by the National Knowledge Commission has studied the situation and made a series of recommendations which the Commission endorsed and submitted to Government in 2007.

Recommendations of the National Knowledge Commission

According to the Commission, some key statistics on legal education are pertinent to understand the state of affairs. The total number of students admitted for legal education in the year 2000-01 is 63,381 and is steadily increasing. They are enrolled in over 750 colleges of which 586 are under private managements and 153 under State Governments. In the fourteen National Law Universities, about 1,500 students receive education. The number of law graduates who enroll themselves as advocates in different State Bar Councils have been steadily increasing from 28,268 in 2002 to 46,438 in 2004. There has been considerable increase in the number of legal periodical and law reports including a dozen online legal databases reporting judgments, Statutes and other legal materials. The pattern of legal practice has also changed from solo practice to law firms specializing in different types of legal and related services. The advent of economic liberalization and globalization under the World Trade Organization not only brought new challenges to the system of delivery of legal services but also enlarged the scope and opportunities for the profession within and outside the country.

In this context, what should be the goals of legal education for tomorrow? One is more confined to the needs of the bar and the bench as it was during the earlier period. Today, it has to meet the growing requirements of Trade and industry, governance at all levels and the unmet legal needs of the society. The National Knowledge Commission felt that legal education must aim at preparing professionals who will play decisive leadership roles in government legislatures, civil services, academia, private corporate sector, international relations, politics and social movements for justice and human rights apart from advocacy in Courts and tribunals. Lawyers have to be in the forefront of movement for sustainable economic development and for ensuring access to justice to all. There is a need to generate new legal tools, ideas and knowledges to support rule of law, good governance and human rights demands.

The vision of legal education is to transform it towards maximizing justice in society and promote the Constitutional goals of a just social order. A spirit of public service must inform and motivate the profession for which legal education should be broad-based in scope, multidisciplinary in approaches and rigorous in analysis and application. The future law persons should be able to deal with international transactions and comfortable with legal systems of other countries. And above all, strong ethical values should inform professional conduct and the system of delivery of legal services.

The task of reform should, therefore, encompass changes not only of curricular and pedagogic arrangements but also the regulatory structure, the pattern of recruitment, funding and management of law teaching institutions.

Curricular reform is a continuing process. The need today is to integrate knowledges across the board to address emerging problems of unprecedented character and dimension. Initially, the 5-year integrated LL.B. course attempted integration of law with social and behavioral sciences. Today, the challenge is to go beyond and try integration with physical and biological sciences to be able to solve problems thrown up by scientific and technological developments. Involvement of trade, industry, civil society and even the student body is necessary to devise and design new core and optional subjects. The Curriculum

Development Committee should have regular feedback from all stakeholder groups and consumers of justice. A model curriculum should be drawn up by the new regulatory authority after adequate consultation for which the institutions teaching law should have freedom to adapt to suit their needs and requirements. An ideal arrangement would be to keep at least half of the total LL.B. curriculum for optional subjects which may be taught in partnership with institutions having special expertise on those subjects. This is to enable students to acquire some degree of specialization which will become necessary in future organization of delivery systems of legal services.

Closely related to curricular changes the method of instruction, Integration demands multidisciplinarity in learning and application. Since the emphasis is on problem solving, the acquisition on multiple skills is as important as the development of substantive knowledge. This requires variety in instructional methods including case study, clinical techniques, project assignments involving research and writing, internships in field offices, seminars, role-plays, etc. To be able to organize and manage such varied instruction on individual basis, the academic calendar has to be developed on a semester or trimester basis. There are distinct advantages if the law school provides residence in campus for all students and faculty so that there is time for co-curricular activities which can supplement and enrich the learning process.

The Common Law Admission Test (CLAT) evolved at the instance of the Supreme Court by the National Law Schools from 2008 can eventually become the basis for eligibility for admission to the study of law. A certain minimum marks in CLAT can be prescribed for admission which may help improve the quality of legal education everywhere.

The revision of the examination system is an essential concomitant of quality improvement under the new curriculum. Examination questions should aim to test capacity for critical reasoning and effective communication. Naturally, questions seeking descriptive answers should be kept to the minimum and problem-solving questions should be more. Evaluation of student performance should be an ongoing process and therefore the tests should be distributed throughout the term. Grades in a five-point or seven-point scale should replace numerical markings and there is no need to fail candidates unless they do not fulfill academic requirements of assignments and class participation. Let the record of the student speak for itself. Allow the student to improve performance if he or she so desires. Educational wastage should be kept to the minimum.

A key issue in legal education which the NKC wanted the law schools to address is legal research essential to generate new knowledge and ideas to transform law into an effective instrument for justice. Research requires a combination of skills which had to be cultivated from the undergraduate level and strengthened at the postgraduate stages. Research enhances the quality of education as well. Keeping in mind the importance of research for the future, the Knowledge Commission recommended at least four autonomous well-networked Centres for Advanced Legal Research in four regions of the country to conduct cutting-edge research on various aspects of law. These Centres can act as think-tank for the governments on emerging legal issues and take consultancy from trade and industry. In association with the law schools, these centres can make research central to learning and practice in law.

Another important issue relates to the appointment and retention of competent faculty for the teaching of a challenging curriculum. There is a severe shortage of teachers as the postgraduate programmes in law (LL.M. and Ph.D.) have long been neglected and the rewards in the teaching profession were not attractive enough for talented scholars. The gap was long managed by induction of practicing lawyers in large numbers into the teaching profession. Full-time teachers were not allowed to practice law or considered for judicial positions. The Knowledge Commission recommended substantial enhancement of salaries to law teachers and better service conditions. Teachers may have to be found from other services where people with law degrees and varied experience in implementation of laws in different sectors are available. They can come as adjunct faculty on negotiated terms. A diversified plan to develop faculty competence and promote retention through incentives should be built into the service conditions. It may be necessary to think of salary differentials within and between Universities and Law Schools.

TOWARDS A NEW GOVERNANCE STRUCTURE

To be able to reconstruct legal education on the lines proposed above, the National Knowledge Commission found it necessary to have a new regulatory authority in place of the Bar Council which will have representation of all consumers of legal services. An independent Standing Committee of 25 members including members of the Bar Councils, Judiciary, Academia, trade and business, social scientists, government representatives can give the necessary inputs to strengthen the regulatory system without sacrificing academic autonomy and professional orientation. This body will set criteria for evaluating law schools in an objective and scientific manner and will rate them in terms of academic excellence. Bar Council of India can administer its own tests if desired for admission to the bar. The scheme of apprenticeship can also be introduced if found necessary by the Bar Council. Judiciary can propose to the Standing Committee on Legal Education what they would want the law schools to facilitate better induction of law graduates to the Judiciary. In fact, the Standing Committee can deliberate and recommend restructuring of different facets of legal education to suit the needs of multiple users of legal personnel and the law school can accordingly decide what they plan to offer. The Standing Committee, according to NKC will consist of a retired judge of Supreme Court, *seven* lawyers nominated by the Bar Councils, seven law teachers, one Government of India nominee, two nominees of trade and industry, one representative of civil society, two persons representing professions other than law, one management expert, one parliamentarian and two final year law students making a total membership of 25.

Financing of legal education should be from multiple sources of which one-fourth can come from tuition fees, State and Central Government funding along with private endowments from industry and civil society should be able to find the rest of financial requirements. However, the pattern will vary depending upon sponsorships and managements. The present trend is to collect 50 per cent or more of the expenses from tuition fees. According to rough estimates of the National Law School expenditures, it is found that an average of ₹ 40,000 to ₹ 50,000 have to be spent on education of a student every year. This does not include capital expenditure on buildings and infrastructure facilities. Self-financing law schools charging annual fee of ₹ 50,000 or more can balance their budget with marginal inputs from endowments and sponsored projects without compromising quality of instruction. This may vary in different locations and with different sizes of student body. The estimates are made on the basis of admission of 80 students per year and one teacher for every ten students.

Continuing Legal Education and the Law Schools

One additional responsibility which the law schools in future will have to undertake is to offer continuing education to legal professionals working in different legal environments and specializations. This has become absolutely necessary with the explosion in knowledge and changing nature of professional services. In fact, it is required for legal academics as well. In organizing continuing legal education programmes for various categories of professionals, the law school will improve its own capacities for the cause of better legal education.

In this regard, Law Schools in future will have to make better use of information and communication technology and learn to economise through cost-effective means of instruction. Distance education is already creating waves in professional and technical studies and there is no reason why it cannot be extended to legal education as well. Distance mode is ideal at least to fulfill the minimum requirements of continuing educaton.

CONCLUDING REMARKS

Education generally is receiving generous financial support from governments today and the private sectors will not be lacking behind as everyone now realizes the importance of good education to sustain growth in a knowledge economy. The idea of public-private partnership is nowhere more relevant than in the field of higher education. The issue today is not so much lack of funds but a proper academic environment in which initiative and enterprise are not stifled by meaningless controls and unhealthy political interferences. Yes, the issue of access and equity are important; but they can be part of the legal-regulatory framework including the reward system for academic excellence. We cannot afford to continue doing things the same way as before as they produce the same result — educated unemployment and unemployability of the degree-holders. In bringing about the desired changes in structure and content, we need to be competitive, looking for models which can effectively combine equity with excellence and equality with competitive spirit.

The next phase of reform in legal education will have to think of the world of 2020s and the role that law will be playing in it and plan a programme of action which can enable the legal system to fulfill the unfinished tasks in the Constitutional agenda of Justice, Social, Political and Economic.

4

Some Comparative Insights From Indian and American Experience

OBJECTIVES OF LEGAL EDUCATION

Preparing students for legal practice is an inadequate explanation of the objectives as legal practice can mean many things in different situations. We talk of litigating lawyers, transactional lawyers, consulting lawyers, public interest lawyers, corporate lawyers, government lawyers, transnational legal practitioners etc., assuming that they do different things differently to achieve different outcomes. While there is some degree of commonality in knowledge, skills and values in all types of legal practice, there are wide variations in approaches, strategies and value systems which condition their varied work as lawyers. There are questions now being asked within the legal community and outside and are engaging the attention of law teachers everywhere.

THE REFORM AGENDA

Among the significant concerns which shape the reform agenda in legal education in India are the following:

(1) Dilution of standards of ethics and professional responsibilities and the failure of legal education to inculcate the right values and professionalism.

(2) The inadequacies in imparting instruction in skills and attitudes which a legal professional is called upon to exercise for negotiating justice within and outside litigation.

(3) The relative neglect of comparative law, international law and conflict of laws in the legal curriculum resulting in the legal community taking a back seat in processes of globalization and development of legal regimes supporting it.

(4) The lack of capacity for integrated and strategic thinking arising from compartmentalized learning and learning at the cognitive level only.

(5) In the context of multiplicity of languages for legal transactions, the issue of language also contributes to the concerns particularly when English continues to play a dominant role in legal discourses.

LIMITATIONS OF CASE-DIALOGUE METHOD

Some Insights from the American Experience

It will be interesting to discuss briefly two recent publications on the subject from United States of America — one from Carnegie Foundation for the Advancement of Teaching on *"Educating Lawyers"* (2007) and the other from the Clinical Legal Education Association on *"Best Practices for Legal Education"* (2007). The Carnegie study is an attempt to interrogate the relevance of the dominant goal in legal education characterized by the idea of *"enabling to think like a lawyer"*. Acknowledging the fact that professional schools set their students apart from others *"by providing systematic involvement into a distinctive knowledge base, binding them into a shared pattern of thinking and acting"*, the report gives credit to the pedagogical power of the so-called case-dialogue method in shaping law students from different social backgrounds in a short period of time with capacities of legal research, writing and argumentation. Compared to other professional fields, which often employ multiple forms of teaching through a more prolonged socialization process, legal pedagogy is remarkably uniform across variations in schools and student bodies. The consequence is a striking conformity in outlook and habits of thought among law school graduates.

The heavy reliance on one "signature pedagogy" to accomplish socialization of young students, the Carnegie report argues results in certain unintended and possibly undesirable consequences. For example, it makes abstraction of the legaiiy relevant aspects of situations and persons from the everyday contexts and tends to give an understanding of doctrines and rules far different from the common sense understanding of lay persons! "Students discover that thinking like a lawyer means redefining messy situations of actual or potential conflict as opportunities for advancing a client's cause through legal argument before a judge or through negotiation." In the process, the role of thinking through the social consequences or ethical aspects of the conclusions remain outside the case-dialogue method.

The report says that if issues such as social needs or matters of justice arise on classrooms, they are almost always treated as addenda and students are told to set aside their desire for justice if they want to succeed in legal practice. "They are warned not to let their moral concerns or compassion for the people in the cases they discuss about their legal analysis." Students have no way of teaming when and how their moral concerns may be relevant to their work as lawyers and when these concerns could throw them off track.

The near exclusive focus on systematic abstraction from actual social context in legal education also lends to unforeseen results such as not focusing on the issues comprehensively and not appreciating the ethical and social dimensions of the profession. Law schools rarely pay consistent attention to the social and cultural context of legal institutions and the varied forms of legal practice.

Whenever these concerns were taken on board, law schools adopted an additive (adding one or two additional courses) approach rather than employing an integrative strategy (of the cognitive, the practical and the socio-ethical aspects), which builds on holistic educational reforms." The goal of greater integration", according to the report, "moans that the common core of legal education needs to be expanded in qualitative terms to encompass substantial experience with practice, as well as opportunities to wrestle with the issues of professionalism."

Vision of an Integrative Model

The major recommendation of the Carnegie report is integration of the student' work experience (apprenticeship and summer employment) in the educational programme (clinical courses particularly) to allow serious, comprehensive reflection with faculty and peers for professional development. In an integrated model, the practical apprenticeship stands not subordinate to but in a complementary relationship with legal analysis. Students need, the report argues, a dynamic curriculum that moves them back, forth, between understanding and enactment, experience and analysis, as they strive to become mature legal professionals. The challenge is developing a model where the cognitive (knowledge-based), practical and ethical-social components of legal education are weaved together in such way that social responsibilities are revealed to the students in context while they imbibe professional skills and develop their legal knowledge base.

"Best Practices" to Provide a Vision and a Road Map

While endorsing the findings of the Carnegie report and building on it, the *Roy Stuckey* study on *Best Practices* commissioned by the Clinical Legal Education Association (CLEA) have "distilled out of the continuing-dialogue a consensus of understanding of an alternative vision of all the components of legal education: an integrated combination of substantive law, skills and market knowledge, and embracing the idea that legal education is to prepare law students for the practice of law as members of a client-centered public profession.: *(Robert Mac Carte, E*sq. in the Foreword to the book on *Best Practices for Legal Education).*

The *"Best Practices"* have been identified based on well-known principles of curriculum development involving four distinct stages; namely, identification of educational objectives, selecting activities appropriate to attain those objectives, organizing the activities in the form of effective instructional modules and designing methods for evaluating the effectiveness of the selected learning experiences. Without a clear defined mission and a plan to achieve that mission, the curriculum of law schools, *Stuckey* argues, remains a collection of activities without coherence and measurable effectiveness of its educational goals. *The Best Practices* book is a clarion call to law schools to clarify and expand their educational objectives, diversify their instructional methods and improve evaluation strategies. It is heartening to find that the book did gather ideas from the experience of the Global Alliance for Justice Education (GAJE) founded in Trivandrum (Kerala, India) in 2000 in a conference of clinical teachers which the author of this article helped to organize towards promoting experiential learning in legal education.

The CLHA study wants the law schools to make an institutional commitment articulating their educational goals and a "shift of emphasis from content-focused programmes of instruction to outcome-focused programme of instruction, law schools should develop knowledge, skills and values progressively and integrate theory, doctrine and practice throughout the three years of law study, in delivering instruction, the study desires that such methods be employed which enable context-based instruction using practicing lawyers and judges". Multiple methods of assessment should be used in evaluating student's learning. Finally, the book wants law schools to regularly evaluate the success of the programme of instruction. The author of the book concludes, "....we are convinced, however, that the major impediment to reforming legal education is a lack of vision and commitment, not a lack of resources."

Indian Experience in Reforming Legal Education

This article is not to introduce the two important US initiatives in legal education reform, but to give some comparative insights on how similar concerns in India resulted in introduction of an integrated Five-year LL.B. programme on an experimental basis two decades ago which, within a short period, changed the course of legal education in the country. In mid 1980s, the experimental programme addressed all the missing links brought out in the two American reports discussed above. As a result, an integrated curriculum for an extended period of five years got introduced as an alternative method of legal education in India. The National Law School, India which was also launched around the same time, helped the experiment in a big way by providing the necessary learning environment of a residential environment of a residential campus and the academic freedom to experiment, innovate and make corrections as frequently as necessary.

Let us elaborate on how the Indian experiment, yet to be completed, offers interesting lessons to some of the concerns and challenges articulated in the Carnegie Report and the CLEA document on legal education. The author's credentials in attempting the comparison is his exposure to the two significant contributions of American System of legal education, namely, the case-dialogue method of instruction and the clinical legal education programme propagated by CLEPK (Council of Legal Education for Professional Responsibility) in the 1960s and 70s. It is not the author's position that the new scheme of Indian legal education is any way superior or worthy of emulation elsewhere; in fact, traditional legal education which is continued in most of law teaching institutions in India is still in a shambles and continues to suffer from all the ills that the two reports have pointed out and more. That is the reason why the Indian experience under the five-year integrated curriculum is said to be still an experiment. However, twenty years is a long period to judge the academic and professional efficiency of the new experiment particularly when more and more governments and institutions are seeking to replicate the Five-Year Integrated LL.B. Programme on the National Law School model. What is written here on that model is not a scientific evaluation of the Indian experiment which awaits expert evaluation; rather it is an insider's response to what have been identified by the American experts as barriers to better legal education.

For purposes of comparison, the following issues in relation to the Indian Experiment have been considered:

1. Integrated Curriculum broadening the objective of legal education and the goals of professionalism.
2. Instructional activities which aim to combine learning of core knowledge, skills and values through integration of theory and practice.
3. Employment of multiple methods (if instruction and best practices using the services of lawyers, judges and social activists).

4. Continuous assessment of student learning through transparent and participatory methods based on objective criterion.
5. Periodical evaluation of the total law school performance by outside experts.

INTEGRATION WITH A VISION

Integrated knowledge is, no doubt, the outcome expected of higher learning. In the case of professional education, the integration is to happen not only in respect of knowledge but also in respect of its application to be able to resolve problems in ethical and socially acceptable ways. Law is a subject eminently suited for integrated learning because of the multiple roles it performs in development of modern societies. The question before legal educators therefore is integration with what, and how, given the constraints of time and resources. The Indian experiment attempted to answer these questions in the following way.

In terms of objectives, while preparing students for legal practice remains the major premise, it is to be acknowledged that legal practice needs to be expanded to include a variety of significant roles that law-trained persons are called upon to perform in governance, in development and in civil society. Such a view of legal practice would require almost all knowledges in appropriate modules to be brought progressively in the teaching/learning of law. This would also require looking at the eligibility qualifications for those seeking to enter the study of law. Naturally, the prevailing three-year period for law study (after a basic degree) is inadequate for the purpose. Therefore, the first step was to increase the duration of the law course to five years and to determine eligibility as higher secondary school examination (which one obtains after 10 years of school and 2 years of pre-university education). In fact, as a next step, the duration should be extended to six years which anyway is the period one would be spending if one were to study law through the alternate programme (i.e., after a basic university degree of three years and then a three-year LL.B. study).

The next question was selection of knowledges for purposes of integrated learning of law in its multiple roles in society. The object was not only integration at the theoretical level but in terms of methods and applications as well. This was indeed a challenging task yet unfinished. It was agreed that this could be done only incrementally. Initially, the law curriculum was designed to include subjects like history, political science, sociology, economics and psychology apart from English language. Later, even physical and natural sciences are to be brought within the curriculum. The relevance and practicality of this move was questioned and some predicted that the experiment is bound to fail in the absence of suitable study materials and non-availability of teachers equipped to teach in an integrative mariner without diluting the objective of legal practice. Space will not permit to describe how this was done in the Five-Year Integrated LL.B. programme at the National Law School, Bangalore, and what are the other outcomes of this experiment. Now, the programme is being extended to more and more law schools and the products are making a distinct difference in legal practice, broadly understood.

For managing such a diverse and expanding curriculum, the National Law School limited the annual admissions to 80 students only and divided the academic year into three teaching terms (trimester) with five subjects of 3 credits each in each trimester. The number of working days in each trimester was 50 or more with each subject receiving at least 80 class hours. There was only a 10 to 15 days' gap between two trimesters within which grades of students were announced. During (the summer vacation of two months, all students were put or, placement (externship) in different locations of their choice. While the first-year students usually go to civil society organizations, political parties and social work institutions, in subsequent years they were rotated in lawyers/judges' chambers, law firms, corporate enterprises, prosecutors' office and legal divisions of Government/Public Sector agencies. There is a lot of flexibility in externships and are not structured excepting a briefing on what to learn, how to use the opportunities to learn and few instructions on personal conduct. They record their experience in a diary which they submit to teachers for comments and guidance. It is assessment of this record and the changes noticed in the quality of interaction of the students which give the faculty a measure of learning they have acquired during externship. No grade is given to students for the externships as they are considered outside the prescribed curriculum and therefore not evaluated. At the same time, these placements during study remain the single-most powerful integrated learning opportunity for students. Besides, for many, it turned out to be a method of choosing their employers in their early career.

Another step in broadening the curriculum was in respect of the range and variety of optional subjects offered from the beginning of the third year of the five-year programme. Nearly half the curriculum consists of optionals. They are so chosen to promote interdisciplinary research-based learning largely through self-study and guided seminars. An element of specialization naturally gets into the scheme of optional curriculum. Furthermore, research and writing skills are tested and refined in this exercise. The quality of papers prepared by students in these courses was so good that many of them get published in Indian and foreign legal periodicals. Some of these optional subjects are developed out of large research projects which the law schools undertake for government or private sector establishments and students get rewarded for their participation monetarily as well. Thus, on an average, National Law School students study at least fifty subjects in five years, some even more, which is almost double the number of subjects a three-year LL.B. students does as per Bar Council Rules. More importantly, they do it in an integrated manner contributing to the development of professionalism and purpose in legal education. The courses on Law and Poverty, Law in Development, Public Interest Litigation etc., give rare social insights into social reality and the laws functioning to generate or ameliorate poverty. This enables the students to ask the right questions in their professional engagements afterwards. The cultural pluralism of Indian society and the social justice concerns of Indian Laws and the Constitution provide ample opportunities for the students to explore areas outside private litigation and discover for themselves why law performs the way it does and what can change it, if desired. Perhaps, the ease with which many lawyers in India move in and out of politics and governance even while they continue in legal practice demonstrate a wider conception of legal practice in Indian social context.

It is also important to point out that under the National Law School scheme, one-third of the credit in each course is given to what is called a project assignment. Project topics are related to the course (though not necessarily so required) and are settled between the teacher and the student at the beginning of the course. The student is expected to write an outline stating (the problem, the issues he wanted to probe, the methodology for it including field visits if any and get the approval of the guide. The final product in the form of a written paper is to be presented in a seminar before the close of the trimester where the teacher grades the performance and advises follow-up action, if required. Writing fifty project assignments in all types of topics in five years' study develops in the student a variety of lawyering skills and value systems in better ways than traditional methods of instruction.

Additional Observations on Instructional Methods and Evaluation

The case-dialogue method, which has not been part of legal education except in Delhi and a couple of other places, became central to the National Law School experiment. It additionally involved the preparing/editing/updating of the study materials for each and every course, making heavy demands on the faculty and the law school resources. As there are still no standardized case books available in India, each law school wanting to teach through case study method has to assemble its own materials. For National Law School, it was a blessing in disguise in as much as it allowed freedom to borrow materials from outside law and integrate it with law study to open up new vistas for legal enquiry. Inevitably, the case method of teaching changed the style of questions in examinations. From mere descriptive and memory-based questions, the examinations came to have problem-type, application-oriented questions, testing skills along with knowledge.

Clinical Methods and Experiential Learning

The status that clinical methods and experiential learning acquired in the experiment is worth mentioning. Again, clinical method is understood here in a more comprehensive sense than is the case in the American situation. For example, the case study discussion, the legal method course in the first trimester, the moot court activity, the project assignment, the summer placement, the legal aid support activities, the community-based law reform activity, socio-legal audit of welfare laws, para-legal work, law enforcement assistance, legal literacy camp, drafting of legal documents, legal research and writing, mentoring of weak students, law journal work, assistance in the preparation of study materials, development of question hanks etc., are all considered part of the clinical programme, whether they come within the required curriculum or outside, whether they are supervised or not, whether they are given academic credit or not. Participation in many clinical activities, some of which sponsored by students themselves, is optional though students try to get involved in as many of them as possible. Instruction for the basic skills as prescribed by the Bar Council is, of course, the law schools' primary responsibility. Beyond that, law school sought to encourage, facilitate and support innovative activities with learning potential without waiting for them to earn a place in the curriculum. Such an approach enabled the law school to be a fertile ground for experimentation and innovation keeping every student involved in number of activities relevant to the community while enabling him to learn the social reality in his own way. The law school assumed greater visibility in society which indirectly helped it to enrich its academic activity through wider networking outside the traditional legal world.

Sustainability of National Law School Experiment

The National Law School experiment was evaluated by an international panel of distinguished law teachers appointed by the Visitor (the Chief Justice of India) who gave a report appreciative of its academic programmes and the quality of its outcomes. However, it was apprehensive of its sustainability at the same level of performance and felt that its success may itself become a source of worry in future. The finding is today shared by many legal educators within the country and outside. Nonetheless, the success of the experiment is today sustained by hundred of its alumni in legal practice all over the world and thousands of students who every year seek to join the institution for their legal education. In fact, law has become a priority option for many bright students because of the NLS experiment. The criticism justifiably raised by a section of lawyers is that the National Law School graduates are not practicing in the lower courts in adequate number nor are they seeking judicial positions. Well, if that was part of the expectation when the experiment was launched, the reasons for its not happening have to be sought more in the profession rather than in the law school.

CONCLUSION

Professionalism is an attitude developed and sustained by the legal practitioners including judges. Unless they themselves put their houses in order, law schools can do very little to influence changes in standards of professionalism in its ranks particularly at the grass roots. Indira Gandhi Open University's School of Law has embarked on an ambitious agenda for legal education through the distance.

5

Legal Education in India and Role of Lawyers (BAR)

1. The modern concept of 'social welfare state' has been affecting national life to a great extent. Under the guise of this concept, the state has now-a-days began to usurp more and more powers, and therefore, not only intervening in the affairs of the society but also attempting to control and regulate the conduct and behavior of the people in the society. This aspect indeed, is a matter of great concern and needs careful consideration in the light of privileges it confers on the one hand and restricts freedoms and liberties to the people on the other.

2. It is an admitted fact that the concept of social welfare state, particularly in all modern democratic countries, has brought tremendous changes and, therefore, constantly generating and promoting the idea of state activism. In consequences, the state activities, to a great extent, is affecting economic, social and political order in the country. The old social, economic and political norms and traditions are giving way to the new complex culture in the society. This indeed, is not a happy trend. The reason is quite obvious. In order to regulate complex relations we need complex laws, and to understand the complex laws we need a skilled and educated class in that discipline. In a democracy like ours where a sizable population is illiterate, the complex laws enacted by the state with a view to promote their welfare, remain ineffective. Not only the illiterate but also an educated man is not in a position to understand the complicacy and intricacy of the complex laws. Ultimately, both the literate and illiterate have to seek advice from an expert in laws. This state of

affairs leads us to the conviction that legal education is necessity of the day in the absence of which the miseries of the toiling mass will remain unremedied. Therefore, legal education and legal profession is the demand of the day.

3. The purpose of the study is to highlight the contribution of the lawyers and those who are directly or indirectly engaged in legal profession, in developing the democratic ideas and their due role in the administration of justice. Simultaneously, an attempt has also been made in this study to identify the causes which are responsible for the devaluation of legal education and professional norms and thereby obstructing the course of fair justice. This is based on the author's personal knowledge of the functioning of the academic institutions at various levels having been in the field of legal profession and legal education for many years.

4. Our history tells us that lawyers have played an important role in attaining independence and developing democratic ideas and values during British period. This was the class who in fact came to the forefront of the freedom struggle and promoted awareness amongst them. In other words, the lawyers have always been in the forefront in all spheres of life, might be political, social and economic. Therefore, they have to act as a leader of the people and guide government directly or indirectly to give society justice.

HISTORICAL PAST

5. When we look upon the history, we find that since beginning legal profession was regarded a noble profession and lawyers were person of proven integrity, character, learning and knowledge of law. Our great saint Narad in his *Dharamsutra* published about 400 B.C. described two types of function of vakil: (a) whether he is authorized or unauthorized could render his legal opinion; if he was law knowing in that case only and (b) such person who was authorized could give legal advice and plead the case for any party. Therefore, it appears that law as a profession seems to have been in vogue in Ancient India. The legal profession as it exists in India today had its beginning in the first years of British rule. The Hindu Pandits, Muslim Muftis and Portuguese lawyers who served under earlier regimes had little effect upon the system of law and legal practice that developed under the British administration.

6. The emergence of the British Empire in India is a decesive event which destroyed the old legal and judicial order to a great extent, and

thus created an environment for the reception and development of English law and judicial culture in the country which later on became our legal creed. In the early days of British settlement, the justice was administered by non-lawyers, and there was also dearth of law knowing men solicitors, lawyers, etc. This state of affairs continued upto 1773.

7. With the establishment of Supreme Court at Calcutta in 1774, practice in law, as a profession came to be recognized, for the first time in India, Clause 11 of the Supreme Court charter empowered the court "to approve, admit and to enrol such and so many advocates and attorneys at law" as the Court shall deem fit. They were to be attorneys of record and were authorised "to appear and plead and act for the suitors" of the Court. The court could remove the said advocates and attorneys "on reasonable cause". No other person whatever, but such advocates and attorneys so admitted and enrolled were to be "allowed to appear and plead or act" in the Court for or on behalf of such suitors. The advocates entitled, thus, to appear were only the English and Irish barristers and members of the faculty of Advocates in Scotland; the attorneys referred to were the British attorneys and solicitors. But an Indian lawyer had no right to appear before the Courts, it was only the Bengal Regulation VII of 1793 which permitted the entry of Indians as pleaders or vakils in the Courts. Therefore, the persons well versed in Hindu and Mohammedan law and persons of character, and education were allowed to enter in the legal profession, and practice law in Sadar Diwani Adalat. Later on, numerous enactments in this regard were passed to regulate the legal profession in India, and at present the Indian Advocates Act 1961 regulates this profession.

EXPECTATIONS FROM A LAWYER: (BAR)

8. Legal profession is a noble and respectable profession. The lawyers, advocates and judges all, therefore, enjoy a pride place in the society by virtue of their character and skill in law and a step further, the services, they render to the society. Their primary function is to solve people's problem and help the poor mass in realising their legitimate dues within a reasonable time. In a democratic set-up, like ours, where the basic law of the land has committed to secure to all of its citizens, justice, social, economic and political and desires to bring a social revolution through legal and constitutional methods, with a view to establish 'Rule of law' and egalitarian society wherein the legitimate aspirations of its people are fully satisfied, the obligations, duties, and responsibilities of a lawyer, which he owes to the community

becomes manifold. These circumstances, therefore, accord to the lawyers an important role of a mediator of the national progress. Therefore, the practicing lawyers are expected to discharge such responsibilities through the legal services they offer to the community. If the lawyers display innovativeness in the use of law and possess insights into the interaction between law and society, the judicial decisions are bound to be forward looking and socially meaningful.

9. The basic duty which is cast upon the lawyer is to fight for the cause of justice maintaining dignity of the profession. The duty of a lawyer is always to place before the judges, and to help them to arrive at, the truth, never to prove the guilty as innocent. The lawyer in discharging his duties shall at all times act freely, diligently and fearlessly In accordance with the wishes of his client and subject to the established rules, standards and ethics of his profession without any inhibition or pressure from the authorities or the public. This short narration makes it clear that lawyers constitute a distinct class in the society and play a vital role in the administration of justice.

LEGAL PROFESSION — A NEED OF THE DAY

10. One of the most outstanding characteristics of the Indian democracy is that, 80 per cent population in our country still resides in villages. Agriculture, being their main occupation, the rate of mobility is very less. Consequently, they are not conscious about their rights and duties owing to their ignorance and illiteracy, and by this reason alone are deprived from privileges and facilities conferred by the State from time to time. Another notable feature is that after independence, the concept of welfare state has given rise to a new culture — complex culture, which causes the state to enact complex laws. Dr. L.M. Singhvi has rightly remarked that:

"Given the complexities of modern society, whatever the stage of economic development in a country, lawyers have became indispensable. Citizens, groups and the state require legal advice at every step to anticipate and avoid problems and to arrange and order their affairs, they require lawyers to represent them. Lawyers have expert knowledge and special skills, what is fundamental, they have a sense of social responsibility, professional ethics, and a degree of independence necessary to the performance of their functions. In modern society, there cannot be a satisfactory or systematic organization of the economic and social activities in a community or in the world (which is itself a community today), and there cannot be an acceptable system of adjudication and settlement of disputes without law or lawyers. Nor can fundamental freedoms and basic human rights be adequately protected and effectively advanced without the active involvement of the legal profession."

The above observation of Dr. L.M. Singhvi appears to be a correct statement of fact. As we find that even an educated person, having sufficient means to protect his interest, rights, etc., finds himself helpless owing to the lack of legal knowledge. Ultimately, he has to seek advice of some law knowing person — a lawyer, so that his grievances could be redressed. It may also be noted that education now-a-days have become more costlier. Consequently, economic condition of the poor mass prevents them to educate their children. Therefore, in the absence of proper education and knowledge, they are unable to protect their rights. To achieve justice is a very difficult task for them. In these circumstances, the duty is cast upon those people who are well to do and well versed in laws. They must come forward and extend their helping hand to mitigate the problems of poor.

DEPARTURE FROM THE PATH

11. The present state of affairs in the legal profession is quite depressing and, therefore, receiving attention of all concerned. The lawyers now-a-days are earning a lot of money from this profession by using tricks, crafty methods and acumen. They charge more than legal fees and do not represent the case in proper way owing to little knowledge of law. The cases and instances of professional misconduct are increasing day by day and, therefore, tarring the image of legal profession.

12. At this juncture, the question arises in the mind of prudent men that what are the causes of failing the standard of legal profession and legal education in our country? Indeed, the standard of legal profession very much depends upon the educational system and its standard. If the standard of education is high, the professional skill and standard will certainly be high. But it is surprising to note that moral and educational values are devaluating rapidly in our country. Therefore, the need is to reorganise the entire educational system and change the educational policies so that the very purpose of the education, may be medical, engineering or legal, could be achieved and the professional skill thus obtained could also be utilized in the interest of community. Shri N.R. Madhava Menon has perhaps rightly observed that:

"The present state of affairs in the legal education front in the country is indeed quite depressing, but not alarming. Of course, part of the malaise is shared by the entire system of higher education and with improvements elsewhere in the system the climate for reform in legal studies also will necessarily improve. If professional legal education demands classroom instruction as well as clinical experience, there has to be reorientation in the content and methods of law courses. The need, therefore, is to identify the issues and problems clearly, determine a frame of priorities in reform and develop alternate strategies and solutions for a phased programme of action. In this effort, the law teachers naturally occupy the leadership role not only in the evolution of policies and programmes but in their sustained implementation with imagination and devotion. After all, the two major pillars of legal education, or for that matter any education, are the teachers and students. Though this truism is often forgotten or overlooked by educational planners and administrators, it is the social and professional obligation of teachers to strive individually and collectively for the better performance of their functions whatever be the structural constraints or institutional difficulties. It is in this belief this paper is written with a view to galvanize the strength of the law teaching community for launching a nationwide effort in reforming the system of legal education to better serve the cause of the profession and demands of socio-economic development."

The above-mentioned observation makes it very clear that the law teachers have to play their due role in maintaining the standard of education. The above observation, also indicates that it is not the institution, that is defective, but the defects and deficiencies are with those who manage that institution. Thus, in this context, the responsibilities of law and also of legal educator assume tremendous proportions, because of the constant need for striking and maintaining a desirable balance between the claims of social regulation and the individual freedom.

6

Standard of Legal Education in India

INTRODUCTION

Legal system in India is the natural outcome of its deep roots in ancient Indian traditions. It has existed in India from the dawn of Aryan Civilization. There are different viewpoints with regard to the genesis of legal education in India. "It is argued that Manu refers to a pleader by the term vipra (Brahmana), from the transaction (Manu VIII 169). This is quite impossible, but we cannot ignore the possibility of the Vipra referred to here being a member of the jury (Sabhya), who might have received an allowance. Dr. Kane also quotes Sukraniti IV 5, pp. 114-17 to say that a person appointed to represent a party should get as his wage 1/16, 1/20, 1/40, 1/80 or 1/60 part of the amount in dispute. K.P. Jayaswal observes that professional lawyers existed in India at least from the time of Manu Smirities. P.V. Kane does not seem to agree with Jayaswal. He opines that there are no evidences which may establish that professional lawyers existed in ancient India. He says that there could be some people who represented others in the King's court, but the opinions of such legal experts were not binding on the king. Dr. Kane has suggested that a person well versed in Dharmashastra and procedure of law could be appointed as the representative. He warned that king should punish any representative who took wages without having these qualifications.

It is quite possible that when the British administration in India introduced a new legal system, some Indian scholars might have glorified the past of India by saying that she already had a well-developed legal system. This is an another matter that it was given a formal recognition by British Government when the first professionship of law was established in Bombay at Elephantine

College in the year 1866 and subsequently the University of Bombay came into existence in 1957 and the Elephantine Law College was affiliated to it. However, we find several references in ancient India where the agents of the party could be father, the brother, the friend, a blood relative, a relative or an authorized agent (Today's lawyers or an advocate) doing some act under the authority of the party. The acts of these authorized agents were binding on the parties who engaged them in their litigation and the decisions by the court under such circumstances were not open to revision, review or retrial. However, Dr. Altekar while agreeing with K.P. Jayaswal also opines that there were advocates in ancient Indian Courts."

At an early date—let us regularly say, at the time of the dharmasutras—professional lawyers or, to be more precise, specialized dharmastrans could not exist. The Indian sage in those days was a specialized in all of the text related to a particular vedic school. His specialized knowledge concentrated on a specific version of the Vedic Samhita and all its related texts; Brahmana, Aranyaka, Upanishad, Srautasurra, Grhyasutra, Dharmasutra, etc. There were no specialists on dharmashastra, and, *a fortiori*, no specialists on law that were part of it. But the situation changed. The texts on dharma grew away from the vedic schools. Gradually, there may have come into being a specialized group of learned men whose main interest was dharma, and the various dharmashastra as such.

There are also sufficient evidence to prove that Legal Professions in India existed even when the first British court was established in Bombay in 1672 by Governor Gerald Angier. The first Attorney General appointed by the Governor was George Wilcox, who "was acquainted with legal business and particularly in the administration of estates of deceased persons and granting of probate." There was much work of this type at Bombay, Wilcox made provision for parties to be represented by attorneys and fixed the "counseler's fee at a little more than rupee one." The record available reveals that at the inaugural procession of the court of judicature there were "fower (four) attorneys or common pleaders on foot". These men were probably Portuguese and Portuguese-Indian, since the Portuguese had ruled Bombay and administered their law there from 1534 to 1668, and Portuguese civil law remained in force under the British until Angier's administration. One of the four, Simeo Sarro (ceron) acted as legal advisor to the company and dominated the court since he was the only one who had legal training and experience. "People were forced to use his advice in difficult disputes. He was so learned in law that he confounded the untrained judges with many references and learned opinions, which they had no way of verifying". He was finally dismissed by the governor for "Cheats" after a petition had been lodged against him.

What is undoubtedly apparent is that parties to a lawsuit in ancient Hindu law had a right to be represented by other persons. The question arises whether or not the representatives referred to in the ancient texts correspond to the pleaders, advocates, vakils or attorneys of modern India. In other words, did ancient Hindu law have the kind of legal procedure in which the rights of the parties were safeguarded through the services of a class of experts, as is the case in present-day India and in most other modern legal systems? Looking at Hindu law, as it became known to the West in the latter half of the 18th century, it did indeed seem as if the question was to be answered in the affirmative. Halberd's code of Gentoo Law (1777), translating the Vivadamavasetu, did have a section (Ch. III and II) explicitly called "of appointing a vakeel (or attorney)". Its reads as:

"If the plaintiff or defendant have any excuse for not attending the court, or for not pleading their own cause, or, on any other account, excuse themselves, they shall, at their own option, appoint a person as their Vakeel; if the Vakeel gains the suit, his principal also gains; if the Vakeel is lost, his principal is lost also."

The study of Rocher Ludo further reveals that Vakeels were not allowed in a cause where the accusation was for murder, for a robbery, for adultery, for eating prohibited food, for false abuse, for thrusting a finger into the pudendum of an unmarried virgin, for false witness, or for destroying anything, the property of a magistrate. The exceptions, however, were where that parties were weak which mainly included a woman, a minor, an idiot, who cannot distinguish between good and evil for himself. The rules appeared to be quite rigid. It is disclosed by the fact that except the brother, father and son of the plaintiff and defendant, if any other person, at the time of trial, should abet, and speak for either party, the magistrate shall exact a fine from him; if a brother, a father, a son, or a vakeel should assist and speak for either party, it is allowed. All this disclose that right from the first translated Sanskrit text onward, scholars were confronted with a picture according to which ancient Hindu law had a system of pleaders similar to the one they were so familiar within contemporary India. The harsh truth remains that though there was no legal education in present form yet there was no doubt, it was being understood in Brhamic form. The manifest object of legal education at that time was nothing but who knew legal proceedings well, was considered qualified for representing as an authorized agent on behalf of aggrieved party and general public and courts accepted him as a pleader or advocate or lawyer's like of today's. Basic qualification for a pleader in ancient time was the full knowledge of Dharmashastra's because rules of law enunciated by the Dharmshastras have been implicitly followed by the rulers of India throughout the milieu as law and have been enforced in courts of law. It is also a hard and undisputed fact that till the advent of the British rule in India, the law laid down by Manu and Yajnavalkya and others have been followed by the courts in India.

STANDARD OF LEGAL EDUCATION IN INDIA

Now-a-days, the standard of legal education in colleges and universities has fallen down to a great extent. The education system in our country seems to have been commercialized. The commercialization of educational institutions in India is responsible to a great extent for the devaluation of educational standard. Therefore, the decline of the professional ideas and ethos led to a virtual collapse of standards and requirements as to education and professional training of lawyers. With due respect and apology, to all those who are directly or indirectly engaged in the processes of imparting legal education in India or elsewhere, an attempt is being made to highlight some of the basic facts and features, which our present-day legal educational system and institutions bears, invariably reserve our attention and therefore, need careful consideration keeping in view the present-day requirements in the best interest of the community.

PRIVATE COLLEGES

To impart education in private colleges is the educational culture of our country. That is why law teaching and professional training is mainly conducted in private colleges all over India. It is a common factor, that four or five lawyers at a tahsil or district headquarters or any other place open law college which is recognised by the university. These colleges enrolled its student in *en masse*, as their main motto is to earn money. To impart education is their secondary object. Law teaching is carried out by part-time law teachers who are mere law graduates. These teachers get very small remuneration for the services they rendered in law college. Being low-paid teachers, they don't take much interest in teaching activities. Their appointments are also made every year. Therefore, there is no security of job as appointments are made on the discretion of the management.

GOVERNMENT COLLEGE AND LAW DEPARTMENT

As we know that there are a few law colleges in India, out of these law colleges a few are run by some of the state governments. So far as I know, in Madhya Pradesh, there is not even a single independent law college. Law, in our state, is being taught in Arts and Science colleges. Law classes are arranged along with other faculties. The law in such colleges is treated as one department instead of one faculty in allotment of funds for purchases of books, equipments and other materials. In some colleges, the building is insufficient to accommodate the classes. The result is that the law classes are held at the convenience of other classes. The number of part-time teachers varies from place to place. The appointments of the part-time teachers are made by the Principal of the college after getting recommended list from the Collector of the state. Here, it may be noted that in case of appointments, of such part-time teachers, the Principal and Collector do not play any vital note except issuing a appointment letter, as the appointment are made on seniority basis. In my opinion, this procedure and practice of appointment of part-time teachers should be changed, and such appointment should be made by a selection board after duly advertising the posts required to be fulfilled on this behalf. In order to attract good advocates, who possess expertise knowledge in any subject, handsome remuneration/honorarium be paid so that the standard of legal education could be maintained. Apart from these part-time law teachers, there should be atleast 50% full-time law teachers with LL.M. qualification.

EVENING CLASSES

Law classes are generally held in evening hours, i.e., 5:30 PM to 9 PM. There are few colleges and departments when law teaching is conducted during daytime, it is either on the morning or in the evening. All that is due to insufficiency of accommodation. The evening and morning classes provide an opportunity to working class to get them educated in law. Therefore, on the one hand, it promotes legal literacy in the country, while on the other, it devaluates the standard of legal education. The reason is quite obvious, that in evening classes the attendance is always poor. The teachers who are engaged in teaching profession are mostly practicing advocates, who have to rush to the college after having tired in the courts. This all affects their teaching efficiency. Apart from this, evening classes do very often create problem to the management and to the students also.

WANT OF CO-ORDINATION IN ADMINISTRATION

As we know that the law department is attached with Arts, Science or Commerce colleges. Therefore, the principal of the college, almost in every case, is of different discipline, i.e., other than law, who governs the law department. He is therefore, not well versed with the gravity of subjects and is always reluctant to manage the department with full vigour and interest. The management also do not extend their sufficient co-operation in managing the affairs of the law department. Consequently, the law teaching is not carried out or conducted seriously which ultimately affects the interest of the students.

ADMISSION ELIGIBILITY

Admission to LL.B. classes is very easy. Anyone who have secured 40% or more marks in graduation is eligible to get admission in LL.B. classes. In Madhya Pradesh, except in Hari Singh Gour University, Saugor, there is no other university or college which is holding pre-admission test to LL.B. classes. That is why any number of students are being enrolled in LL.B. classes without having considered the other aspects, such as, accommodation, teachers and the library facilities. The liberal admission rules, are to some extent, responsible to promote the idea of commercilization of educational activities and simultaneously, in devaluating the standard of legal education all over the country. S.S. Kulshresth has perhaps rightly observed that,

"The meritorious students of Arts, Science or Commerce pursue higher studies in their respective faculties. The result is that 80 to 90 or 95 per cent of students having lower percentage of marks join this course. They join course not because they want to join legal profession but only to pass their time while seeking employment somewhere-else or preparing themselves for other competitive examinations. Some students can be hard by saying that they come only to lead college student life. This is because of lack of effective control over admissions and other defects in the admission system."

Therefore, the need is to check the inflow of number of students to LL.B. classes. It is submitted that the present admission system be reformed and amended keeping in view the value of legal education and its contribution in developing the law and legal system in the country. Law teaching and education is not any less important than Medical or Engineering. It is also one of the branches of knowledge. If medical education and medical services are essential to keep the health of citizens, the legal education and legal services are equally essential to maintain just social order in the country. Therefore, it is necessary that some positive steps should be taken to admit only those students who have keen interest to study law and have made up their mind to practice law thereafter.

RELAXATION IN ATTENDANCE

Although Bar Council of India has made it compulsory that a student should attend 75% lectures during an academic session to make him eligible to appear in the examination. In most of the cases, it is seen that attendance is either supplied by another student or in cases where the attendance of a student is less than 75% the managing authorities do not take care of it. This state of affairs, established the fact that the rule regarding attendance of students are not being observed strictly. We have our own experience that the student, who has not attended 75% of lectures, is not detained from appearing in the examination, due to the fear that the student so detained adopts illegal means and attempts to pour force on the authorities against his detention. Therefore, in such circumstances, it is not possible to prevent or detain law students whose attendance is short. Relaxation in attendance has now-a-days became their privilege.

PATTERN OF QUESTION PAPERS

Being a law teacher, I have abundant experience that the present system of setting the question papers is not free from defects. As a matter of prudence, the question papers are required to be prepared by a law teacher who has expertise knowledge of the subject. But in practice, we find that things are altogether different. What the paper setter does, he often collects some model question on the subject and prepares the question paper. Sometimes, it is found that there are questions which are repeated in verbatim every year. This pattern indeed, promotes the ideas of "selected reading and limited teaching." But this does not mean that intelligent questions are not being asked in the examination. There are teachers, but rare in number, who possess the quality and ability to put an intelligent question in the paper by which the degree of knowledge of an examinee is tested. Therefore, it is desirable to introduce some change in the present pattern of question papers so as to enlarge the scope of study otherwise, the very purpose of legal education would be defeated.

EVALUATION OF ANSWER BOOKS

Now-a-days, the system of 'central valuation of scripts' is widely prevalent, which indeed, is a time-bound programme. The valuation work is therefore carried out in hurry and haste. Therefore, the scripts of the examinees are not valued properly, which in turn promote discontentment amongst the students. The dissatisfied students very often rush for revaluation of their answer books. That is why the cases of revaluation of answer books show upward trend every year, which in fact not only affecting the carries of students but also creating administrative problem and thereby keeping the teachers, busy in evaluating the answer books throughout the year. The faulty system of evaluation of answer books of the examinees sometimes spoils the academic carrier of intelligent students and increases mental agony, the loss of which is irreparable.

THE METHOD OF TEACHING

In almost all the colleges, law is being taught in a classroom by delivering lectures by a teacher. But now the age of old lecture method has bygone, it has certain demerits of which we must take cognizance The lecture method, therefore, ought to be replaced by some other method, e.g., case law method, group discussion method and the like. The case law method and group discussion methods provide an opportunity to the student to express himself and to offer fair comments on the subject. The object of these methods is to impart extensive as well as intensive knowledge of law. Some audio and video means, if adopted, would certainly yield good results.

LACK OF LIBRARY FACILITIES

The position of law library in law colleges is not very sound. There is always dearth of good textbooks in the library. New books are not purchased due to inappropriate allotment of funds. The library remains almost closed during daytime due to insufficiency of staff. Inadequate library facilities thus deprive the students to access the good books.

Although the aforementioned state of affairs depicts a dismal picture of legal education and legal profession in our country. This has, indeed, happened due to improper functioning of the educational institutions. For the devaluation of standard of legal education and professional norms, a large number of factors are responsible, of which the most important are social, economic and political. Economic and political instability in the recent past has generated numerous problems which were hitherto been unknown in our country, the State's interference in every walk of national life is also an alarming event. Therefore, these events not only instruct but also remind all of us to play our due role so that a just social order could be maintained in the country. But the question before us is how to overcome this problem? What is the effective means or instrument by which a social order can be maintained in society? To my mind, the answer to the above questions, is only to put life into law and legal system both. Law in modern times, is regarded the only effective means and also a powerful instrument by which, if not all but many social, economic, political and national problems can be resolved. Therefore, it is high time to activities to all concerned who are engaged in imparting legal education, and justice delivery system and inspire them to participate in the process of strengthening law and legal system in the country.

It will be appropriate to quote Chief Justice Gajendra Gadkar who in his inaugural address to the Kasauti, Seminar on legal education (1964) observed that,

"In a democratic society, which is dedicated to the cause of establishing socio-economic justice, law offers to merely a command of the legislature. Law becomes a dynamic weapon in the armoury of democracy to achieve its objective of reaching the ideal of a welfare state. As soon as law ceases to merely a command, and assumes the role of a flexible instrument intended to serve the cause of socio-economic justice, it follows that the study and teaching of law must also change their complexion."

Therefore, the need is to reorganise the system of legal education so that a well-skilled class of lawyer is produced who will fight for the cause of justice and thereby restore the reputation and prestige of noble profession. Therefore, the quality and usefulness of legal profession very much depends on the ability, skill and intelligency of law teachers and the method by which the law education is being imparted in the colleges and universities. If the feedback of lawyers is good, the justice delivery system would certainly be efficient and effective, as the corpus of judicial organ is formed amongst the eminent lawyers of the bar. This situation establishes the fact that education is the very foundation of legal profession on which depends the success of a justice delivery system. The objectives of legal education, legal profession and justice cannot be translated into practice unless the instrumentalities by which the functions of these institutions are performed, do not realize their responsibilities and discharge duties and obligations in true sprit and sense, to which they are committed. With a view to make the system workable, the following points are suggested.

(i) The private colleges where the number of full-time teachers are less than 50% should not be permitted to impart legal education.

(ii) Handsome remuneration/honorarium be paid to the part-time teachers.

(iii) The law colleges should be independent.

(iv) Pre-admission test at the state level should be held each year.

(v) The admission rules should be adhered strictly.

(vi) 75% attendance should be made compulsory. Any relaxation in this regard should not be allowed.

(vii) Unified syllabus for all law colleges should be prepared by the Bar Council of India.

(viii) The pattern of questions should be based on practical problems and questions of law.

(ix) There should be provision of training at least for two years.

(x) Audio and Video means should be made available for effective teaching.

(xi) Model answers should be supplied to the evaluator to enable him to access the correctness of answers.

(xii) Adequate library facilities should be made available.

(xiii) The scheme of 5-year degree courses should be implemented.

Although many armchair deliberations both, at the State and National level have been held but they could not yield any fruitful results. Indeed, it is high time when we should adopt some positive steps so that men be trained in laws for the prosperity of the nation and to have rule of law in the country.

7

Teaching Techniques in Legal Eduction – A Critical Evaluation in the Light of Changing Social Scenario

INTRODUCTION

India is a vast country with complex and varying systems with diversified interests in the way of socio-economic living. But the culture and heritage inherited from times immemorial are binding on the people of India to stand on unity and integrity. This has also been possible because the fact that an average Indian respects voluntarily to ethical and moral values as being the harbingers of Natural Law as compared to the provisions of man-made laws or inhibitions, and that for enforcement of the principles ethics and morality there is no need for the establishment of any supervisory and enforcement authorities unlike the enforcement of man-made laws. In view of the increasing patterns of internationalization of the educational policies and programmes, the objective of education, especially the higher education, is shifting from traditional techniques to modern hi-tech patterns aimed at achieving self-centered economic enrichment and privileged living. Growing information technology is adding fuel to the fire.

Now it is well recognized universal norm that, of all the educations, legal education gains significance in the eradication of socio-economic inequalities, assurance of human rights with dignity and decency, and in combating all other social ills and evils that are long inherited by people out of the "Law of Jungle".

Since the advent of University-based law schools, legal education has been facing the challenge of reconciling its aims and objectives from time to time in accordance with the changing needs of the society and moods of the people at the helm of affairs. Today, the law and order situation in the country is out of track. Crime rate is growing abnormally. Respect to law and legal system is narrowing down. State and its machinery are not able to control and regulate this abnormal state of affairs in the deserving manner. Thus, it is high time to think about appropriate remedial measures to meet this urgent and growing danger. The answer is obvious; we need an effective law and legal system. This is in turn is possible only if the Universities produce ideal and efficiently skilled law graduates. This in turn requires an ideal and effective teaching tools and techniques certain exceptions, the teaching techniques adopted in the Universities are largely restricted to classroom methods and examination patterns, thereby making students half-hearted and half-knowledged. The teaching tools available to teachers and students are too ineffective to properly achieving the targeted goals.

Keeping the above aspects in view, the present article is developed. It identifies the problem areas and also provides for appropriate solutions suiting the present-day needs and future aspirations.

TEACHING TECHNIQUES

(a) General Aspects

Before discussing about the concept of "Teaching Techniques", it would be subtle to substantiate its meaning. "Teaching" means to teach a subject in question. "Techniques" means the scientifically developed methods. Thus, the phrase "Teaching Techniques" envisages teaching of a subject in a question by means of scientifically-developed methods. A method of teaching developed scientifically is one, which can be applied at all levels of teaching of that subject uniformly. But today, teaching techniques, especially in countries like India, are mostly based not on any scientifically-developed norms or principles, but on the individual whims and fancies of the teachers in question. In fact, it is a problem area to identify as to what type of teaching technique is adoptable to what type of subject study. It differs from subject to subject and place to place depending upon the receiving end products.

Today, in India, each University has had its own syllabi and its own teaching techniques. There is no uniformity. As a result, the standard of education differs from state to state and institution to institution. It all depends upon various factors, which are well-known amongst the academicians. This equally applies to legal education.

In general, the teaching techniques of today include, *inter alia,* planning of teaching schemes, preparation and supply of teaching material, if any and teaching the subject in the classroom. Most of the times, such teaching will have no relevance to the practical needs of the students as also the outside world. As a result, the products coming out of the Universities find no parity with their knowledge acquired in the University education and the practical problems that they are going to encounter in their employment or day-to-day life. Thus, there is need to provide for appropriate remedial measures to meet this situation.

(b) Teaching Techniques in the Legal Education

It is beyond argument that the teaching techniques to be followed in respect of legal education are entirely different from those of other professional subjects. Teaching techniques in legal education address particular courses and clinical studies. These envisage message-sending capabilities to the community committed to creating resources to meet the socio-economic challenges in and out of the country and help eradicate the suffering created by the abuse of law and misuse of power by the people at the helm of affairs.

Teaching techniques in legal education aspire preparing students to competently practice law, perfectly understand legal issues incorporated into core curriculum courses. Law teachers who are not familiar with these techniques will obviously produce ineffective products, which will reflect negatively on the entire gamut of legal system and judicial activity. These techniques must train the recipients of legal education to acquire skills and efficiencies sufficient to provide solutions to all social problems. This is possible only if there are comprehensive core curriculum courses in the legal education.

Today, Legal Education is aspiring certain new developments, such as the demand for more specialization, more practical in training, more problem-based teaching, and assured employment opportunities at national and international level.

Although curriculum and syllabi for various subjects of law are prepared and followed keeping in view the above aspects, but in practice and subject always to certain exceptions, the picture is entirely different, *inter alia* for the following reasons:

1. lack of experience and expertise among the law teachers,
2. lack of infrastructure, tools, equipment and academic atmosphere in and around law schools,
3. lack of practical professional experience among law teachers,
4. lack of encouragement to teaching faculty from the appropriate authorities,

5. least attention to legal research and development,
6. groupism and corruptive practices among teachers, students and authorities in teaching, evaluation and awarding,
7. lack of interaction to identify ways and means for meeting the changing patterns, needs and remedial measures to practical problems,
8. placement of ineffective and inefficient persons in effective and key positions,
9. political interference in academic matters,
10. violation of Rules and Standing Orders by the people in helm of affairs, and
11. growing absenteeism amongst the students and lack of interest in studies.

AUTHORITIES GOVERNING THE LEGAL EDUCATION

Legal education in India is presently governed and controlled by the following fivefold institutional network:

1. Universities imparting legal education,
2. Bar Council of India,
3. University Grants Commission,
4. Private Educational Institutions affiliated to any University, and
5. The Government at Centre and States, as the final authorities.

A perusal of the functioning of all these Institutions goes to show that each one has got its own programmes and policies and would like to show their supremacies over the other. As a result, there is no due and proper attention towards the area of teaching techniques and their timely upgradation. The entire job is left to the authorities at the bottom of the hierarchy — the Departmental level. In the absence of requisite supervision over the bottom level departments, the standards of legal education are gradually coming down.

(i) Relevance of Different Teaching Methods

(a) **Teaching at Classroom:** As already mentioned, there are no scientifically-developed teaching methods especially in law schools established by or affiliated to the Universities imparting various other courses of study. The commonly followed teaching method is teaching the subject matter in the classroom as one-way traffic. This has gained significance owing to the growing absenteeism among students. The number of students present at the classroom in vast majority of colleges will hardly be 10 to 20 per cent. The subject curriculum included for teaching is over flooded. Similarly, the number of subjects for the entire course is being increased from time-to-time, thereby paying least attention to important legal subjects, especially in respect of procedural laws. In such a situation, the teacher, however, he might possess advanced teaching techniques and other skills, will have no zeal to teach appropriately. What is taught is generally the subect material available in the books and least attention is paid to explain the relevancy of that subject to the practical life and social set-up. The teaching is aimed at completing the syllabus and preparing the students for examination, and not for making them as useful and skilled citizens.

The teaching techniques adopted for the discourse of practical papers like Moot Courts, Practical training, Drafting of suits, Writs and other proceedings is not at all up to the mark. This area has become more or less fanciful to fulfill the curriculum requirements. As a result, law graduates are injected into the society without efficiency and expertise to enter into the profession of law or other legal employments as knowledgeable sources.

The present teaching method is not followed by the student participation and student-teacher interaction. In fact, the vast syllabus incorporated in each subject does not permit the teacher to allow student participation in the day-to-day teaching exercises in the deserving manner. Nor does it widen the mind of the students to receive variety of subjects in a short span of academic time schedule.

(b) **Teaching Outside the Classroom:** Teaching at outside the classroom in the existing spectrum of legal curriculum includes Court Visits, Moot court competitions, Practical training at Advocate's chambers and court visits, etc. If these practices are strictly adhered to, obviously the Universities can produce ideal professionals. But unfortunately, these are allowed to be done only formally to fulfill the curriculum requirements without planning for concrete results and evaluating the standards of individual students.

(ii) Evaluation

(a) **Of the Students:** The existing system of teaching techniques does not give pace to the classroom evaluation. The time earmarked for the teaching the subject is barely enough to complete the syllabus, and a teacher will neither have time nor zeal to evaluate the student performance at classroom.

The evaluation of student performance is visible only through the examinations. Even such evaluation does not appear to be always the obvious method, for various reasons. Evaluators are most of the time will be those who will have neither taught the subject, nor did any academic activity in relation to it. As a result, the evaluation of a particular subject by those who have no knowledge of it leads to negative and discouraging results, thereby depriving the confidence and reliability on the examination system as a whole.

(b) **Of the Teachers:** The evaluation of the performance of teachers by the students, although forms part of the teaching techniques, is not strictly adhered to. Even if any evaluation is obtained from the students, it will reflect only the interest of the administrative heads in-charge of the affairs in relation to the concerned teacher. As a result, it has become theoretically impossible to practically evaluate the performance of teachers.

(iii) Establishment of Professional Teachers' Training Centres

As far as the subject of Law is concerned, in the existing system there are no professional teachers' training centers, except those of institutions undertaking conduct of Orientation or Refresher Courses. In fact, these courses have been oriented to use for obtaining requisite eligibility to the next promotion, rather than practically imparting additional skills and knowledge amongst the teachers. The institutions, which are imparting such courses, engage as resources persons amongst such of those who are either the friends or relatives of the organizers or others who can influence the organizers. They never have the zeal to ascertain the experts in a given subject. As a result, whatever is done at the said Centres has become more formal than practical. There are also no criteria as to which teacher can be sent for what Orientation or Refresher Courses and everything ultimately dependent upon the whims and fancies of the Principal concerned.

The other problem is that neither there is sufficient number of Professional Teacher's Training centers, nor any policy or programme to that expectation. No such zeal appears to be present even amongst the teaching community. If at all any teacher wants to participate in any such teacher training programmes, he will have to be away from his place of work and home, inasmuch as the duration of such courses always exceeds a fortnight.

(iv) Conditions of Service for Teachers

The existing conditions of service for teachers is not up to the expectations, especially among those engaged in private educational institutions, who are discriminated in various ways as compared to those employed by Universities. Senior Teachers with higher contribution and greater experience are equalized in many ways with the juniors, and sometimes juniors are placed in such positions whereby they can control, threaten and deprive the other benefits of the seniors. This is a pathetic situation.

(v) Incentives to Teachers

The existing system does not have pace with incentives to teachers. The only incentive for sincere teachers is that of a 'Good teacher' off the record. The promotional or other benefits are time-targeted and no additional benefits are offered for any additional academic work. The additional administrative work, such as performing the duties of Principal, Vice Principal, etc. assigned to teachers are extended to only such persons who are in the good looks of the higher ups unconnected with any other criterion. This is of course a worldwide phenomenon, especially in countries like India.

(vi) Introduction of Adjunct Teachers (Lawyers and Retired Judges)

In India, it is generally seen that professional knowledge and expertise/ experience is used only for achieving greater economic goals. Maybe because of this, the lawyers and retired judges who expect higher remuneration is neither invited for sharing their knowledge among the students as adjunct teachers nor they are willing to do so on their own. In view of dearth of the requisite number of teachers, junior lawyers are often invited to act as adjunct teachers, but practical experience goes to show that they are unable to deliver the requisite goods and services, for various reasons.

(vii) Student Attendance — Linkage of It with Examination

Almost all universities, other than Law Universities, complaints of poor percentage of attendance in classrooms is a common phenomena. There are various reasons for this bad state of affairs. The major reason for this problem is poor and inefficient administration. In the existing set-up, attendance is linked with the appearance of examination, but students who have not attended even a day are allowed to write examination by manipulating the attendance. It is not an exaggeration, if mentioned that even persons in Government full-time employment are often allowed to complete the course of study as full-time students and are awarded degrees. There will also be persons doing more than one course during the same academic year. There is no proper check or machinery to do so, for eradicating this illegal practice.

CONCLUSIONS AND SUGGESTIONS

From the foregoing discussion, it would be seen that the existing state of education in general and legal education in particular is in tutelage. Educational institutions are established for imparting ideal education. It is obvious that better working conditions will attract better teachers. Better amenities will ensure better students. Competent teachers will produce competent citizens. Therefore, it is necessary for all to maintain discipline and abide by the rules and regulations. Ideal education is the requirement of the day. At this stage, it would be appropriate to note the observations of the University Education Commission appointed as early as in 1948, under the Chairmanship of Dr. S. Radhakrishnan, in relation, *inter alia,* to include matters relating to means and objects of university education and research in India and maintenance of higher standards of teaching and examination in Universities and Colleges:

"It should free us from the shackles of ignorance, prejudice and unfounded belief. If we are incapable of achieving the good life, it is due to faults in our inward being, to the darkness in us. The process of education is the slow conquering of this darkness."

In view of the above, it would be appropriate to make the following suggestions for the present purpose:

1. A working chart of teaching techniques to be adopted and followed by all the Universities shall be prepared and circulated for adherence and it must be ideal, congenial, and enforceable by all teachers.
2. The existing curriculum of law course shall be revamped — relevant aspects are included and irrelevant excluded — in such a way that it should not overburden neither the teacher nor the students, but inspire them to develop practical knowledge.
3. A minimum of three year's practice as a lawyer must be made as an additional essential qualification for the appointment of a law teacher.
4. Right persons shall be appointed in right places so that proper evaluation — of teachers and students — can be made at and outside the classroom level and at examination level.
5. Additional incentives must be given to the teachers with higher qualification, experience, and contribution in teaching, research and development.
6. Teachers engaged in Private Colleges shall be extended the benefit of equal remuneration on par the teachers of Universities with all other amenities and facilities.

7. Teachers must be given appropriate training including training in using the Computer and Internet techniques and equipment; opportunities to obtain higher qualifications, and to achieve multi-subject knowledge.

8. Attendance of students must be made mandatory for writing examinations and the erring persons must be subjected to some disciplinary action.

9. More number of Teachers' Training Centres shall be established manned with persons of high caliber and commitment with a view to update the knowledge and skills of teachers with modern and internationally-acceptable teaching techniques.

10. In the last, it may be said, "Let not a teacher teach out of the fear or want of livelihood, but for the overall development of the students and the institution".

8

Road Map Ahead

LEGAL EDUCATION

Significance of Legal Education

In a modern, civilized, democratic and political state, as the India is, it is the law of the laws – the Constitution of India, which has conferred freedom on us, the right to live with human dignity and conscience. Widespread and deeply pervasive network of the laws leaves hardly any human activity outside its net which is not governed by some law or the other. Birth, death and marriage have to be registered. There are laws on how to move or drive on the road, how to travel, where to smoke or not to smoke, what to eat and what not to eat, where to go and where to refrain from going and so on. The air which we breathe, the water which we drink and the food which we eat, the house in which we live in, whether rented or owned, are all governed by some or the other law. From a little child purchasing a rubber or a pencil, to an adult travelling by air within or outside country – all are subject to some law. Law determines the boundaries of human behavior which determines the limits of transgression as well as compliance. Everyone is supposed to know the law and the ignorance of law does not excuse anyone. So pervasive, complex and fast changing are the laws that a car bumper read "Do it today, tomorrow it may be illegal", such is the pace of today's existence.

Many Jurists have tried to define law and one such definition is – "Law is nothing but rules of morality, ethics and common sense codified: In a democratic society, it is said that laws are collective will of the people expressed through legislature. The Supreme Court has ruled that **'rule of law'** is a basic feature of the Constitution. In short, if we have to live, we can live only by law. Education in law enables the citizens learning their rights and duties. A society enlightened by law can be most effective in shaping the nation and putting a check on abuses and misuses of laws. It can lay foundation of a nation whose citizens love justice, are law abiding and believe in just and lawful coexistence for all the members of the society. Howsoever just be the laws enacted, they cannot be effective in delivering effective societal justice unless they are put into action by professionals well versed and well instructed in law. Hence, the justification for legal education is not only for those who wish to take law as profession but also for those who wish to be responsible and enlightened citizens of a free nation. To learn the law, everyone need not be required to go to a law school. Elementary knowledge of the basic laws and Constitution should be imparted to all students at secondary level of education. Mahatma Gandhi and several martyrs laid down their lives to earn the freedom. We have to preserve it. Thomas Jefferson, former US President, once remarked: "If a nation expects to be ignorant and free, it expects what never was and never will be." Education alone can erode ignorance. The UNESCO charter states: "Since wars begin in the minds of men, it is in the minds of men that the defenses of peace must be constructed."

J.S. Rajput, Director, NCERT has stated in one of his articles that the entire world is talking today of fighting against the terrorism of various kinds – social, racial, economic, colonial, military, etc. "The only right weapons and approaches would be information, knowledge and wisdom. All other weapons have outlived their utility. These are the days of mind power. Right education is the key to peace and prosperity."

The legal education has two purposes to achieve: (i) it shapes enlightened and responsible citizens of a democratic nation; (ii) it equips an aspirant to enter a profession which is one of the highly respected and lucrative in the world.

Legal Education

The pressing need to do something about the legal education as it is administered at present has been engaging the attention of almost everyone concerned with the legal profession, particularly after independence. At various forums and in articles, the matter has been debated. Committees have also been appointed from time to time to recommend reforms in legal education. The general pattern of education has also been undergoing a constant attempt at restructuring and improving, with the result that general education and legal education have remained in a state of uncertainty.

Those who have been trained in the former system of education and have begun their practice during the pre-independence days and have continued their practice till the seventies have seen a vast change coming over the field of legal practice, and the kind of litigation coming up in the Courts. Apart from the explosion of litigation, during the post-independence era the variety of litigation and its kind has undergone a sea change. The equipment possessed by the lawyers and jurists or academicians who were responsible for administering the legal system has been found to be ill-suited and insufficiently armed for the flood of both the litigation as well as legal education requirements in other walks of life. For a legal system geared to deal with crimes of the ordinary kind under the Indian Penal Code, and property and personal laws, we have a new broad spectrum of subjects or litigation. Even so on the horizon of today's system of legal education, there is very little change. Far from being in step with the changes coming along, it has remained more or less static.

Need for Change in Legal Education

There has been a general and gradual fall in the standards both in general education and more so in the legal education. With the opening of a large amount of avenues and vistas for talented young men in all walks of life after the independence, the law has ceased to attract the cream of intelligence. Today's lawyers, as one observes functioning in Court, are woefully ill-equipped with the instrumentalities of a legal practice. Apart from the knowledge of law, the general equipment for the profession is difficult to find, leave aside qualifying for a successful practitioner. What we see today is acquired by few on account of the skills possessed by them sharpened by experience at the cost of their clients.

Our legal system has been attuned on the model of the Anglo-American system and jurisprudence. The experience gained there would therefore be of some use to us also. In the United States, Carnegie Commission was appointed to study the legal field. It found that while the subjects engaging the attention of the former lawyer were real property and commerce, subsequently and particularly in the larger cities, the industry and the large commercial organizations became his customers. The profession changed to some extent from advocacy in courts to practice in Chambers in an advisory capacity. That again got itself concerned with the increased legislative control over the national economy and intervention of the Government in normal life. And today there is a considerable growth of specialization in the legal field.

Formerly, a degree was a must before entering a law school. The acquisition of a professional qualification could be had 2 years thereafter it was 3 years after graduation. This process, therefore, meant 16 years of college and school life before a person could take to any of the legal careers. This was after 4 years of the primary school, 7 years of secondary school and 4 years of college education.

Governance and Implementation of Legal Education

The present Law courses and Legal Education is governed by Bar Council of India Rules and the Advocates Act, 1961. The relevant provisions are enumerated below:

Bar Council of India Rules:

Section 7(1)(h) **The functions of the Bar Council of India shall be —** to promote legal education and to lay down standards of such education in consultation with the Universities in India imparting such education and the State Bar Councils.

Advocates Act, 1961:

CHAPTER I

2. **"Definitions"**

2(v) **"Degree in Law"** means a degree conferred by the University recognized by the Bar Council of India for the purpose of the Act, after successfully completing study for not less than three years or an integrated bachelor degree combining the courses of a first degree in any subject and also the law running together in concert and compression for not less than a period of five years after 10+2 or 11+1 school course as the case may be.

CHAPTER II

4. Law Courses. There shall be two courses of law leading to Bachelor's Degree in Law.

(a) **A Three Years' Unitary Degree Course:** A three-year course in Law undertaken after obtaining a first degree from a university or any other qualification considered equivalent qualification by the Bar Council of India.

Provided that admission to such a course of study for a degree in Law is obtained from a University whose degree in Law is recognized by the Bar Council of India for the purpose of enrolment.

(b) **A Double Degree Integrated Course:** A double degree integrated course combining first degree course with the degree course in law, which shall not be less than five years' duration leading to the combined and integrated degree in the respective discipline of knowledge and Law together.

Provided that such an integrated degree in Law of the University is recognized by the Bar Council of India for the purpose of enrolment.

Explanation:

In the case of integrated double degree course, the entire double degree course can be completed in one year less than the total time required for regularly completing the two courses one after the other in regular and immediate succession, meaning thereby, that if the degree course in the basic discipline such as in Arts, Science, Social Science, Commerce, Management, Fine Arts, etc. is of three years' duration of studies, integrated course in Law with the first degree in the discipline could be completed in five years' time but where the first degree course in basic discipline takes four or five years in Engineering, Technology, Medicine etc., the integrated degree in Law with first degree course in the discipline would take one year less for completing in regular time than the total time taken for the two degree taken separately if completed back to back.

Eligibility for Admission:

(a) A person may apply for admission in a three-year degree course in law if any of the following conditions is fulfilled:

   (i) Obtained the first degree in any subjects from a University or

   (ii) Any other equivalent qualification recognized by the UGC AICTE or any other body established for the purpose and approved by the Bar Council of India.

(b) a person may apply for admission in the integrated course in law on fulfilling any of the following conditions:

   (i) Passed Senior Secondary School course ('+2') or equivalent qualification such as 11+1, 'A' level in Senior School Leaving certificate course from a Board constituted or recognized by the Union or by a State Government or

   (ii) Pre-University course from a University or

   (iii) Equivalent qualification as recognized by the Union or the State Government as the case may be or any other body established for the purpose and approved by the Bar Council of India.

Prohibition to Register for Two Regular Courses of Study:

No student shall be allowed to simultaneously register for a law degree course with any other graduate and postgraduate or certificate course run by the same or any other University or an Institute for academic or professional learning excepting in the integrated degree course of the same institution.

Provided that any short period programme for a period not exceeding one year part-time certificate course on computer course or computer application of an Institute or a Centre for Distance Learning of a University, however, would be excepted.

Minimum Marks in Qualifying Examination for Admission:

Bar Council of India may from time-to-time stipulate the minimum percentage of marks to be obtained in the qualifying examination such as higher secondary examination in case of integrated course or first degree examination in case of unitary course for the purpose of applying for admission in a law degree course in a University without prejudice to any University or Center for Legal Education prescribing higher minimum marks in the qualifying examination.

Provided such minimum qualifying marks shall not automatically entitle a person to get admission to an institution, but the candidate should also fulfil other institutional criteria notified by the institution concerned or by the Government from time to time as the case may be, in this regard.

Standard of Courses

All Universities and its Centers for Legal Education conducting either the unitary three years' degree law course or the integrated five years' double degree course or both would follow the outline of the minimum number of law subjects both theoretical and practical, compulsory and optional, as the case may be, prescribed by the Bar Council of India and specified in the Schedule 11 on the recommendation of the Legal Education Committee, the University shall ensure that:

(i) The minimum number of law subjects are effectively taught in the Centers for Legal Education with adequate infrastructural facilities as may be prescribed and in the manner stipulated by the University Rules and Regulations and Rules of the Bar Council of India.

(ii) The minimum standard of first degree courses in the case of 5-year integrated course as designed and run by the University for that purpose of the standard prescribed by the University in view of the academic and other standards laid down, if any, by the standard-setting institutions like University Grants Commission or All-India Council of Technical Education or any such body, as the case may be, and the course is effectively run with adequate number of faculty in respective subjects, with infrastructural facilities as may be prescribed by that standard-setting institution as well as the Bar Council of India, and

(iii) There is a regular and proper evaluation system for the purpose of certification of the students graduating in law after completing the course as a regular registered student.

Process and Manner of Running Integrated Course

The University concerned shall ensure that:

(a) Faculty for running the entire course shall design the purpose, manner and the process of running the integrated courses semester-wise with clear objective criteria of integration.

(b) There are all infrastructural facilities available for the courses, such as faculty for teaching the subjects concerned, laboratories needed, and other classroom fixtures and fittings including the computer support as prescribed by the Bar Council of India from time to time.

Provided that the University for the purpose of Rule 9(a) shall submit annually to the Bar Council of India copies of the curriculum designed and developed in each subjects of study, rules of academic discipline and of examination and evaluation. The Bar Council of India would review the courses from time to time and provide suggestions to the University concerned, if any.

Semester System:

The course leading to Degree in Law, either on unitary basis or on integrated double degree system, shall be conducted in semester programme with not less than 30 hours' input per week over a period of not less than 15 weeks classroom teaching in each semester in case of unitary course and 18 weeks classroom teaching in the integrated course.

Minimum Infrastructure:

Any Centre of Legal Education conducting legal education by running either of the law courses or both leading to conferment of graduate degree in law on successful completion of the course shall have minimum standard infrastructure facility stipulated by the Bar Council of India specified in Schedule III of these Rules.

The University shall also ensure that all its Centres of Legal Education maintain the prescribed minimum standard infrastructure and other facilities.

Final Semester Test:

No student of either unitary or integrated course in law shall be allowed to take the final test in the semester in any subject unless the student concerned has attended minimum of 70% of the classes held in the subject concerned as also including the moot court from exercise, tutorials and practical training conducted in the subject.

Provided that if a student for any exceptional reasons failed to attend 70% of the classes held in any subject, the Dean of the University or the Principal of the college, as the case may be, may allow the student to take the test if the student concerned attended at least 65% of the classes held in the subject or subjects but attended 70% if classes in all the subjects taken together and also including the moot courtroom exercises, tutorials and practical training conducted in the subject.

Provided that a list of such students allowed taking the test with reasons recorded be forwarded to the Bar Council of India.

Prohibition against Lateral Entry and Exit:

There shall be no intermediary degree awarded to any student in an integrated double degree course and there shall be no lateral entry during any year within the integrated course. The only entry point in an integrated double degree course is in the first year and only exit point for awarding an integrated degree is at the successful completion of the 5th year, i.e., on the completion of entire double degree course.

Thus, the above-mentioned rules may be summarized as follows:

There has now been a change in the system of education all over, with an intention to standardize the pattern of education all over the country. That new pattern is the pattern of 10 plus 2 plus 3. If after these 15 years of education, one has to spend 2 or more years for acquiring the necessary skills for legal career, then a prospective student would have to spend a minimum of 17 years. It seems it is now necessary to consider the desirability of legal education taking over as an independent stream or discipline right from the college years. If that were done, entry to a legal career will be open after 10 plus 2 course. Subjects may be added and joined as optional subject for persons choosing as their objective a legal career at that level on the plus 2 pattern. After three years of college education for a course-oriented, to equip people wanting to take up a legal career, a primary degree like the other systems and disciplines should be possible. This would permit a student to pick up his future career in any of the other walks of life and compete himself for the job market where those various organizations like the companies, banks, corporations, local authorities would be able to recruit him. Those concerned and interested in professional career connected with the legal practice in Courts or tribunals, and before authorities can be placed under the control of the All-India Bar Council acting through the Central Committee, while the higher careers in legal education to remain with the Universities.

Skills Training in Legal Education

Legal education should be more skills-oriented and here a brief reference is made to the role of clinical legal education and other skills important in legal education.

Methods of Instruction

(a) Talk and Chalk Tradition

The dominant method of law teaching in India, which I call the talk and chalk tradition, involves a close analysis of the statutes and their interpretation given by the courts. Students are given lectures, sometimes supplemented by tutorials, introducing them to the broad principles of a particular subject with potted versions of leading cases, which they are then expected to follow up themselves. Lecturing, note-taking, memorizing, mugging and regurgitation in once-year examinations are the hallmark of the talk and chalk tradition. The yearly examination is changed to Semester pattern for both 3-year and five-year integrated programme.

The talk and chalk tradition is however not indigenous: it is a mutilated form of traditional English method of teaching law. But law in England was always regarded as a practical subject; it is still the case that a law degree is only a first step to qualification, for prospective lawyers must undergo "internship" for a further period completing professional examinations before they can be admitted to bar. An important difference with England has been that the profession in India has never been able to establish its own training on a firm basis. The old apprenticeship did not work here because of various reasons – seniors never had no time to supervise pupils, they interviewed and negotiated with clients, not the pupils, no or meager allowance was paid, and so on.

The talk and chalk tradition is not as unintellectual as sometimes suggested, although learning tends to take precedence over thinking. The better teachers teach students **the tools of legal analysis – thought, reasoning** and the **application of principles to new situations**. Overall, however, this method leads to a form of legal training where teachers and taught are mainly concerned with "chopping logic with judges and passing their opinions". The line between legal and extra legal matters is carefully drawn, and the products of talk and chalk tradition profess a strict celibacy when it comes to temptations like policy. Law teachers are completely devoid of practical training though they often claim to combine the two – academic and practical training.

(b) The Case Method

Developed by the then Dean of the Harvard Law School (C.C. Langdell) at the turn of the present century, the case method, like the talk and chalk tradition, focuses largely (and sometimes, solely) on only one aspect of law — the decisions of mainly appellate courts. Langdell took the view that law was a matter of studying the cases, just as scientists proceeded from the particular to the general, so the law student had to start with the cases and then to formulate principles. However, the case method took root as Harvard graduates multiplied and went on to populate American law schools. When in early sixties Indian law graduates and teachers began visiting and obtaining S.J.D.'s from United States law schools, rather than British Universities, they brought back to India the case method and the so-called Socratic technique of teaching it.

The initiators justified case method on various grounds. Cases have always featured prominently in common law system, in contrast to the continental system where codes are pivotal. The expanding body of case-law necessitates an emphasis on learning technique rather than on substantive knowledge which is constantly changing. The Socratic method of case-teaching, whereby teacher and students engage in a joint examination of the principles of cases, is supposedly more satisfying and provides a greater intellectual challenge than where students sit passively faithfully noting down lectures which must then be rote learnt.

Both the talk and chalk tradition and the case method have been adopted in Indian legal education one after the other, although many deficiencies crept into them in the process of adoption. The talk and chalk tradition, an inheritance from British, was followed without the essential fusion of academic and practical training; the case method, an inheritance from Americans, without "Cases and Materials: This is besides the fact that the British and the American methods are both deficient in that they focus largely on case-law. Cases are but one aspect of law, and those prescribed and discussed are unrepresentative of those which go to trial. Not only that the law reports contain an unrepresentative sample of cases initiated (students therefore do not know about disputes settled informally), the cases studied are usually very few and those too of appellate courts. Law students thus become experts on the largely irrelevant and unusual penumbra areas of legal disputation without having much knowledge of the core of everyday legal activity."

(c) The Skills Orientation

It is very sad fact that both the talk and chalk traditions and the case method are largely irrelevant to what the great majority of law students will eventually do. Some of the bright ones might be of use to well established lawyers who practice before appellate courts, but others are an inadequate preparation for the average lawyer. Most lawyers spend a great deal of time in interviewing clients and negotiating with other professionals, but when a fresh law graduate goes to the court he literally lands, like a man coming down in a parachute, in a foreign country of new and exotic environment that requires a high degree of specialized knowledge and experience. Training is also absent in other essential skills like investigating facts, drafting documents, conducting a trial and legal research.

Three main changes are suggested to correct the present orientation of legal education. *Firstly,* law teachers must have greater experience in practice so that they can teach courses designed for the needs of practice. *Secondly,* students must be compelled to study a wide range of subjects, additional to the basic subjects (contracts, torts, property, criminal law, and so on), such as conveyancing, company law, trusts, procedure, moots and taxation. It is alarming to think that a student who passes out from a law institution has not done moots at all. *Thirdly,* students should receive instructions in skills like drafting, interviewing and negotiation, it is here that clinical legal education assumes importance.

(d) Clinical Legal Education

It is obvious that skills cannot be taught in the abstract by academics. It is to achieve this that clinical legal education needs to be introduced. Students can only truly appreciate law if they carefully observe what goes on in courtrooms and lawyer's chambers. Clinical law will get students out in the real world, via clinics, to see and learn how lawyers actually operate. They will be taught to see the interaction of the conduct of society and their work of its courts and lawyers. It is earnestly hoped that clinical law would correct certain undesirable tendencies in contemporary legal education. For instance, it will serve as a half-way house between prolonged isolation in the classroom and the outside world and contribute to the development of realistic values.

If clinical law is to be justified, then, we must go beyond the skills argument to the deficiency in legal services in the community. It is in meeting the legal needs of the poor that legal education through clinics has its vocation. Despite recent efforts to develop legal services for the poor the demand is still largely unfulfilled. Clinical legal education-oriented to the poor means that students concentrate on certain aspects of law and develop legal skills hitherto neglected in Indian legal education. Poor people do not want to establish family trusts to avoid taxation, rather their legal problems, which the wealthy few will not experience will revolve around family, housing, consumer, criminal and social service law.

Meeting the unmet legal need in the community has been the main thrust of clinical law in the affluent countries like the United States, Australia and Britain, where the law schools have harnessed the enthusiasm and idealism and desire for relevance on the part of how students to the valid social purpose of ensuring adequate legal services for those who cannot obtain them. That immediate steps need to be taken in the Indian law schools also in this direction requires no emphasis.

Autonomous Law Schools in India

Autonomous Law School in India were founded in 1984 with an attempt to improve legal education throughout India.

First foundings

In 1984, there was felt a need to professionalize the legal sector of India. Legal luminaries like I.N. Mitra, Prof. Menon, etc. decided upon the novel idea of National Law Schools to be set up with the financial assistance of State governments but retaining autonomy in all other respects. This gave rise to the National Law School of India University (NLSIU), Bangalore established in 1988 by Prof. Menon which was the first national law school to provide integrated course in Law.

Later additions

Later colleges like NUJS, NALSAR, Gujarat National Law University, Gandhinagar, National Law University, Jodhpur, Hidayatullah National Law University grew up to fill up the vacuum. The most recent aditions of national law schools are Ram Manohar Lohia National Law School, Rajeev Gandhi National Law University and RNLU and others.

Programme

This pioneering 5-year integrated degree model of legal education wherein students pursue the study of law at the undergraduate level after finishing high school (10+2) and is awarded a B.A. or B.Sc. degree along with the LL.B. degree, was a reformative attempt to rejuvenate the flagging quality of legal education in India. The success of this model of legal education has inspired the formation of may other "national" law schools all over India. This model has been seen largely as being successful in increasing the quality of lawyers. Though there still remain many criticisms of the employment pursuits of the graduates of these institutions, which is seen as being focused on corporate law firms and companies rather than the bar, academia or social service. This has in many ways defeated the idealistic objectives like "social engineering" or "justice education" and the ultimate aim of creating lawyers service the disempowered masses of India.

A few tips to the law students to be successful in profession –

(i) Work hard

(ii) Be physically fit

(iii) Value the time

(iv) Knowledge of English language

(v) Read literature

(vi) Knowledge of Computers and technology

(vii) Develop a hobby

(viii) Look smart

(ix) Aim High

LEGAL PROFESSION

Studying of Law for a career

To the students of law, I would like to emphasize a few issues.

Law as a profession in the 21st century and with a march in the field of globalization has ceased to be a traditional profession. The days are gone when taking instruction in law could be an evening pastime. There were part-time teachers. Attendance could be by proxy and learning by heart a few questions and answers from guides or solved papers for a month or two before taking examination, could suffice for passing. Mostly practice in law was considered to be hereditary where son having got a degree in law would inherit his father's lucrative practice and continue the same for good or bad. Now, with the introduction of National Law Schools and five-year full-time law courses, law is a specialized field of education. All good law schools and colleges have introduced entrance examinations where students are admitted by competitive test and on merit. Clinical education having been imbibed into course of study a degree in law dispenses with need for practical training afterwards. A degree-holder in law is almost equipped to embark into practice just as his counterparts in medical profession, engineering or chartered accountancy. With the indulgence shown by the Bar Council of India, armed with statutory power given to it by the Advocates Act, 1961, course of study in law is so designed as to meet the requirement of those who wish to take profession seriously by aiming at becoming lawyers and not by chance. Education in law is no more an option of last resort. It is now a coveted course of professional education.

A conventional lawyer used to develop more or less personal relationship with the client. He would be engaged by client to draft a plaint or a written statement and to act or plead for him only Court of law. There were trial and appellate lawyers. In any case, their activities were confined to Courtroom preceded or followed by consultation and study in chambers or residential office. Now the role which a lawyer assumes is of a policy planner, a business advisor, a negotiator between groups having common interests, an expert in articulation and communication of ideas, a mediator, a lobbyist, a law reformer. With the widening horizons in the field of litigation and hitherto unknown fields entered into by lawyers and Courts of law such as sustainable development, environment sciences, cyber space law, genetic engineering, professional negligence, international legal disputes and intellectual property matters, one cannot think of becoming a successful lawyer solely by learning the law. He has to learn allied sciences and sources of knowledge of bio-diversity and biotechnology is a must. To draft documents and treaties with international ramifications, the lawyer ought to have a command over language and learn the art of articulation. All this requires a wide range of learning, continuing education and choosing the field of practice wherein one would like to specialize.

The globalization far-reaching ramifications on legal profession which has also increased the pace and complexity of law practice. This many lawyers who cannot cope to leave practice. Globalization has also increased the mobility of lawyers with the rig skills and experience. Many lawyers are practicing in offshore law firms in the major financial centers of the world. We too, domestic lawyers can move to law firms located here, and litigation lawyers can move sideways to non-litigation arbitration. In the last few years, many senior advocates have been devoting more time to arbitration practice, especially

Lawyers as Professionals

There was a time when a lawyer was regarded as a family friend. He commanded awe and respect. And for good reasons. Prominent freedom fighters belonged to the legal fraternity and played a leading part in the framing of our Constitution. Gandhiji, Pandit Nehru, Dr. Ambedkar, Alladi Krishnaswami Iyer, K.M. Munshi to mention just a few. Lawyers gave up their practice to join the freedom movement and many of them went to jail in the cause of the freedom struggle.

At present the public image of lawyers is far from flattering. They are seen as fortune seekers rather than seeking to serve a selfish class, who, on account of their special knowledge and expertise, provide services on such terms as they please. In short, the profession of law is regarded as a money making racket. Today people are apt to agree with Dean Swift's description of lawyers as, 'a society of men bred up from their youth in the art of proving by words multiplied for the purpose, that white is black and black is white according as they are paid." No longer is the profession of law regarded as a noble one.

What are the reasons for this said decline? The main reason is that lawyers, as also other professionals like doctors for example, have forgotten what is entailed in a profession and their proper role in society.

It is forgotten that the essential difference between business and a profession is that while the chief end of business is personal gain, the main goal of a profession is public service.

Apparently lawyers have forgotten that they are the guardians of noble ideals and traditions, and not mere traders in the market-place, whose sole aim is the amassing of vast fortunes.

It is not suggested that lawyers should not charge for their services and charge well in heavy matters where there are corporate clients. A lawyer needs to make money like any other person, and is not expected to live on love and fresh air. But his main purpose and desire should be of rendering service to those who seek his aid and also to the community of which he is a necessary part. To those unable to pay adequately, or not at all, professional service should be freely and cheerfully given. If doctors can have free medical clinics why should lawyers not run free legal clinics at least once a week? Lawyers must devote some part of their time and services free of charge for the benefit of the poor and the oppressed.

The legal profession has a social dimension. And the lawyer has a social role to play in society. The social dimension becomes a very relevant issue when we look at the manner in which legal services remain by and large inaccessible to the common person, particularly in a poor country like ours.

The assumption of our legal system is that all citizens have equal access to means of legal redress. Access to inexpensive and expeditious justice is a basic human right. In practice, legal services of all kinds have gone to the highest bidders. Wealthy persons and large corporations receive the highest quality advice. The poorest in the society, the "third world population", receive negligible or very haphazard and poor legal advice. The term "third world" is used as an all-inclusive expression for the exploited elements of society, the minority groups, the workers, and the peasants. It also includes society's "deviants" — prisoners, mental patients, radicals, dissenters as well as the powerless groups generally, such a youth, women and the disabled.

There are rare exceptions to this rule also.

A lawyer because of his importance in society and the respect that is accorded to the black gown he dons has certain obligations to discharge both inside and outside the Court.

Lawyers to whom Providence has been kind and have established a lucrative practice and have benefited from the profession should not decline the call to serve on the Bench unless there are genuine compelling domestic or personal reasons. Of course, there will be a reduction in the income and also restriction on social and other activities which are inevitably entailed upon elevation to the Bench. But some amount of sacrifice should be made as part of the moral obligation of a lawyer to serve the society and the profession of which he has been beneficiary. There is one admonition which I may be permitted. After accepting judgeship do not grumble about the fall in income and do not bother about how much the leading members of the Bar are earning.

There is one more aspect to which I wish to advert. Senior lawyers have an obligation to train and encourage junior members of the Bar and should not deny entry into their chamber to juniors who are keen to learn and have a commitment to practice law. A competent well-trained junior Bar is an essential adjunct to the administration of justice. The role of a senior lawyer is not merely to familiarize the junior with case law and the relevant statutes. The habit of independent thinking and questioning should be inculcated. And, above all, the junior must be exposed to an imbibe the noble traditions of the Bar, the tradition of truthfulness, the tradition of fearlessness, the tradition o fairness and the tradition of service to the indigent and the disadvantaged.

It was the boast of Emperor Augustus that he found Rome of brick and left it of marble. But how much nobler will be the lawyer's boast when he shall be able to say that he found law dear and left it cheap; found it a sealed book and left it a living letter; found it the patrimony of the rich and left it the inheritance of the poor; found it the two-edged sword of craft and oppression and left it the staff of honesty and the shield of innocence.

I am an unrepentant optimist. I have no doubt that if we dedicate ourselves to the realization of that noble vision not by mere words but by deeds and by practicing the noble profession of law in the spirit of public service we shall restore the stature, the dignity and the image of our profession and play our rightful role in society and provide much needed service to the community and become a model for emulation to others.

Changing Face of the Legal Profession in India

Globalization brought about a revolution in international trade with increasing participation and involvement of countries and greater access to domestic economies. The implication of the same on the legal service sector has been both qualitative and quantitative.

The emerging legal service sector is equally beneficial to all the consumers of legal services, without discrimination. In the age of consumerism and completion law, consumer's right to free and fair competition is paramount and cannot be denied by any other consideration. Trade in legal services focuses on benefits accruing to consumers from legal services sector, particularly the quality of service available with respect to particular fields.

Regulations on Trade in Legal Services Hampering Growth and Development of the Sector

1. In India, there is an absolute bar on advocates advertising and soliciting for any purpose, and indicating any area of specialization.
2. The Bar Council of India Rules, 1975, in Chapter III, Rule I, prohibits advocates from entering into partnership or any other arrangement for sharing remuneration with any person or legal practitioner who is not an advocate.
3. The regulatory and legal system in India has the effect of limiting the size of legal establishment.
4. In India, only natural persons can practice law, as is evidenced by combined reading of Sections 24, 29 and 33 of Advocates Act and artificial body cannot act as a lawyer.

   Opening up of legal services sector is going to lead to a flow of expertise in sectors where local firms and lawyers are deficiently delivering services. Accepting 'trade' of legal services would develop the profession qualitatively.

About Profession

The job of a lawyer is to assimilate and analyze facts quickly and to identify and distinguish the relevant factors from the irrelevant in a given situation. He should also have a good command over written and spoken language and should be able to present matter in a clear and precise manner.

Today, it is the practice of commercial law and especially the field of corporate law and international trade law that is quite beneficial and lucrative. Apart from all these, taxation laws, constitutional law, patent law, labour law, family law, mercantile law, contract law, administrative law are all areas which are both interesting and rewarding. Some lawyers may prefer to specialize in handling civil suits or handle criminal matters as they find it more challenging.

Whatever be the nature of the specialization that is taken up, in order to be successful in the practice of law, one should have a basic law of the Indian legal system.

A few frequently asked questions (FAQs) on the Indian legal system are given below:

- What are the sources of law in India?
- Who can make laws in India?
- What is the hierarchy of Courts in India? How are the Courts in India organized?
- Who can be classified as an advocate?
- What does the Advocates Act 1961 provide for?
- What is the difference amongst Senior Advocate, an Advocate on Record and an advocate?
- Who is responsible for maintaining a record of all advocates in India?
- What are the qualifications for enrolment as an advocate?
- What are the kinds of law degrees recognized by the Bar Council of India?
- Can a person with a foreign law degree be enrolled as an advocate in India?
- What are the disqualifications for enrolment?
- Who is a Notary? What are his functions?

A few thoughts for kind consideration of those who wish to join the profession:

(i) Restore the lost glory of profession

(ii) Self-discipline

(iii) Memorize, modernize and march ahead

(iv) Develop second line/next generation

(v) Social Service and charity

Annexure - I

THE ADVOCATES ACT, 1961 (ACT XXV OF 1961)

(Then Act printed here is as on 27.2.1979)

CHAPTER I
PRELIMINARY

1. **Short title, extent and commencement.**—(1) This act may be called THE ADVOCATES ACT, 1961.

(2) It extends to the whole of India.

(3) It [shall in relation to the territories other than those referred to in sub-section (4), come into force] as the Central Government may, by notification in the Official Gazette, appoint, and different dates may be appointed for different provisions of this Act.

(4) This act shall, in relation to the State of Jammu and Kashmir and the Union territory of Goa, Daman and Diu, come into force on such date as the Central Government may, by notification in the Official Gazette, appoint in this behalf, and different dates may be appointed for different provisions of this Act.

(a) Substituted for the words "It extends to the whole of India except the State of Jammu and Kashmir", by Act 60 of 1973, S. 2 (31.1.1974).

(b) The Act has been extended to—

(i) the Union territory of Dadra and Nagar Haveli by Regn. 8 of 1963, S. 12 (1.7.1965); and

(ii) Union territory of Pondicherry by the Pondicherry (Extension of Laws) Act, 1968 (26 to 1968).

(c) Sub-section (4) inserted by Act 60 of 1973, S. 2 (31.1.974).

2. Definition.—(1) In this Act, unless the context otherwise requires—

(a) "advocate" means an advocate entered in any roll under the provisions of this Act;

(b) "appointed day", in relation to any provision of this Act, means the day on which that provision comes into force;

(c) Omitted;

(d) "Bar Council" means a Bar Council constituted under this Act;

(e) "Bar Council of India" means the Bar Council constituted under Section 4 for the territories to which this Act extends;

(f) Omitted;

(g) "High Court", except in sub-section (1) [and sub-section (1A)] of Section 34 and in Sections 42 and 43, does not include a court of the Judicial Commissioner, and, in relation to a State Bar Council, means—

(i) in the case of a Bar Council constituted for a State or for a State and one or more Union Territories, the High Court for the State and one this into or more Union territories, the High Court for the State;

(ii) in the case of the Bar Council constituted for Delhi, [the High Court of Delhi],

(h) "law graduate" means a person who has obtained a bachelor's degree in law from any University established by law in India;

(i) "legal practitioner" means an advocate [or vakil] of any High Court, a pleader, Mukhtar or revenue agent;

(j) "prescribed" means prescribed by rules made under this Act;

(k) "roll" means a roll of advocates prepared and maintained under this Act;

(l) "State" does not include a Union territory;

(m) "State Bar Council" means a Bar Council constituted under Section 3;

(n) "State roll" means a roll of advocates prepared and maintained by a State Bar Council under Section 17.

(2) Any reference in this Act to a law which is not in force in the State of Jammu and Kashmir or in the Union territory of Goa, Daman and Diu, shall in relation to that State or that territory, be construed as a reference to the corresponding law, if any, in force in that State or that territory, as the case may be.

(a) Section 2 renumbered as sub-section (1) thereof by Act 60 of 1973, S. 2 (31.1.1974].

(b) Omitted by Act 107 of 1976, S. 2 [15.10.1976].

(c) Omitted by Act 60 of 1973, S. 3 [31.1.1974].

(d) Inserted by Act 60 of 1973, S. 3 [31.1.1974].

(e) Substituted by Act 60 of 1973, *ibid.*

(f) Substituted by Act 107 of 1976, S. 2 [15.19.1976].

(g) Inserted by Act 60 of 1973, S. 3 [31.1.1974].

CHAPTER II
BAR COUNCILS

3. State Bar Councils.— (1) There shall be a Bar Council—

(a) for each of the States of Andhra Pradesh, Bihar, Gujarat, [Jammu and Kashmir], Madhya Pradesh, Mysore, Orissa, Rajasthan and Uttar Pradesh, to be known as the Bar Council of that State;

(b) for the States of Assam, Manipur, Meghalaya, Nagaland and Tripura and [the Union territories of Mizoram and Arunachal Pradesh, to be known as the Bar Council of Assam, Nagaland, Meghalaya, Manipur and Tripura];

(c) for the State of Kerala and the Union territory of Laccadive, Minicoy and Amindivi Islands, to be known as the Bar Council of Kerala;

(cc) for the State of Tamil Nadu and [the Union territory of Pondicherry to be known as Bar Council of Madras;]

(ccc) for the State of Maharashtra and [the Union territories of Dadra and Nagar Haveli and Goa, Daman and Diu] to be known as Bar Council of Maharashtra;

(d) for the States of Punjab and Haryana and the Union territory of Chandigarh, to be known as the Bar Council of Punjab and Haryana;

(dd) for the State of Himachal Pradesh, to be known as the [Bar Council of Himachal Pradesh];

(e) for the State of West Bengal and the [Union territory of the Andaman and Nicobar Islands], to be known as the Bar Council of West Bengal; and

(f) for the Union territory of Delhi, to be known as the Bar Council of Delhi.

(2) A State Bar Council shall consist of the following members, namely:

(a) in the case of the State Bar Council of Delhi, the Additional Solicitor-General of India, ex-officio; [in the case of the State Bar Council of Assam, Nagaland, Meghalaya, Manipur and Tripura, the Advocate-General of each of the States of Assam, Manipur, Meghalaya, Nagaland and Tripura, ex-officio; in the case of the State Bar Council of Punjab and Haryana, the Advocate-General of each of the States of Punjab and Haryana ex-officio] and in the case of any other State Bar Council, the Advocate-General of the State ex-officio;

(b) in the case of a State Bar Council with an electorate not exceeding five thousand, fifteen members, [in the case of a State Bar Council with an electorate exceeding five thousand but not exceeding ten thousand, twenty members, and in the case of a State Bar Council with an electorate exceeding ten thousand, twenty-five members, elected in accordance with the system of proportional representation by means of the single transferable vote from amongst advocates on the electoral roll of the State Bar Councils;]

[Provided that as nearly as possible one-half of such elected members shall, subject to any rules that may be made by the Bar Council of India be persons who have for at least ten years been advocates on a State roll, and in computing the said period of ten years in relation to such person, there shall be included any period during which the person has been an advocate enrolled under the Indian Bar Councils Act, 1926].

(3) There shall be a Chairman and a Vice-Chairman of each Bar Council elected by the Council in such manner as may be prescribed.

[(3A) Every person holding office as Chairman or as Vice-Chairman of any State Bar Council immediately before the commencement, of the Advocates (Amendment) Act, 1977, shall on such commencement, cease to hold office as Chairman or Vice-Chairman, as the case may be:

Provided that every such person shall continue to carry on the duties of his office until the Chairman or Vice-Chairman as the case may be, of each State Bar Council, elected after the commencement of the Advocates (Amendment) Act, 1977, assumes charge of the office].

(4) An advocate shall be disqualified from voting at an election, under sub-section (2) or for being chosen as and for being, a member of a State Bar Council, unless he possesses such qualifications or satisfies such conditions as may be prescribed in this behalf by the Bar Council of India, and subject to any such rules that may be made, an electoral roll shall be prepared and revised from time to time by each State Bar Council.

(5) Nothing in the proviso to sub-section (2) shall affect the term of office of any member elected before the commencement of the Advocates (Amendment) Act, 1964, but every election after such commencement shall be held in accordance with the provisions of the rules made by the Bar Council of India to give effect to the said proviso.

(6) Nothing in clause (b) of sub-section (2) shall affect the representation of elected members in any State Bar Council as constituted immediately before the commencement of the Advocates (Amendment) Act, 1973, until that State Bar Council is reconstituted in accordance with the provisions of this Act.

(a) Inserted by Act 60 of 1973, S. 4 [31.1.1974].

(b) Omitted by Act 26 of 1968, S. 3(1) and Sch. Pt. I [10.6.1968].

(c) Omitted by Regn. 8 of 1963, S. 12(2)(i) [10.6.1968].

(d) Substituted by Act 81 of 1971, S. 34 [21.1.1972].

(e) Inserted by Act 26 of 1968, S. 3(i) and Sch. Pt. I [10.6.1968].

(ee) Original clause (cc) relettered as clause (ccc), *ibid.*

(eee) Substituted by Act 53 of 1970, S. 25 [25.1.1971].

(f) Substituted by Act 60 of 1973, S. 4 [31.1.1974].

(g) Substituted by Act 81 of 1971, S. 34 [21.1.1972].

(h) Inserted by Act 60 of 1973, S. 4 [31.1.1974].

(i) Substituted, *ibid.*

(j) Inserted by Act 21 of 1964, S. 2(b) [16.5.1964].

(k) Substituted by Act 38 of 1977, S. 2 [31.10.1977].

(l) Inserted by Act 21 of 1964, S. 2(c) [16.5.1964].

(m) Inserted by Act 60 of 1973, S. 4 [31.1.1974].

4. Bar Council. (1) There shall be a Bar Council for the territories to which this Act extends to be known as the Bar Council of India which shall consist of the following members, namely:

(a) the Attorney-General of India, ex-officio;

(b) the Solicitor-General of India, ex-officio;

(bb) Omitted;

(c) One member elected by each State Bar Council from amongst its members.

[(1A) No person shall be eligible for being elected as a member of the Bar Council of India unless he possesses the qualifications specified in the proviso to sub-section (2) of Section 3].

(2) There shall be a Chairman and a Vice-Chairman of the Bar Council of India elected by the Council in such manner as may be prescribed.

[(2A) A person holding office as Chairman or as Vice-Chairman of the Bar Council of India immediately before the commencement of the Advocates (Amendment) Act, 1977, shall, on such commencement, cease to hold office as Chairman or Vice-Chairman, as the case may be:

Provided that such person shall continue to carry on the duties of his office until the Chairman or the Vice-Chairman, as the case may be, of the Council, elected after the commencement of the Advocates (Amendment) Act, 1977, assumes charge of the office].

(3) The term of office of a member of the Bar Council of India elected by the State Bar Council shall—

(i) in the case of a member of a State Bar Council who holds office ex-officio, be two years from the date of his election [or till he ceases to be a member of the State Bar Council, whichever is earlier;] and

(ii) in any other case, be for the period for which he holds office as a member of the State Bar Council.

Provided that every such member shall continue to hold office as a member of the Bar Council of India until his successor is elected.

(a) Clause (bb) omitted by Act 38 of 1977, S. 3 (30.10.1977).

(b) Inserted by Act 60 of 1973, S. 3 (30.10.1977).

(c) Substituted by Act 38 of 1977, S. 3 (30.10.1977).

(d) Inserted by Act 21 of 1984, S. 3 (10.5.1964).

(e) Inserted by Act 60 of 1973, S. 5 (31.1.1974).

5. **Bar Council to be body corporate.**— Every Bar Council shall be a body corporate having perpetual succession and a common seal, with power to acquire and hold property, both movable and immovable, and to contract and may the name by which it is known sue and be sued.

6. **Functions of State Bar Councils.**— (1) The functions of a State Bar Council shall be—

(a) to admit persons as advocates on its roll;

(b) to prepare and maintain such roll;

(c) to entertain and determine cases of misconduct against advocates on its roll;

(d) to safeguard the rights, privileges and interests of advocates on its roll;

(e) to promote and support law reform;

(ee) to conduct seminars and organise talks on legal topics by eminent jurists and publish journals and papers of legal interest;

(eee) to organise legal aid to the poor in the prescribed manner;

(f) to manage and invest the funds of the Bar Council;

(g) to provide for the election of its members;

(h) to perform all other functions conferred on it by or under this act;

(i) to do all other things necessary for discharging the aforesaid functions.

(2) A State Bar Council may constitute one or more funds in prescribed manner for the purpose of—

(a) giving financial assistance to organise welfare schemes for the indigent, disabled or other advocates;

(b) giving legal aid or advice in accordance with the rules made in this behalf.

(3) A State Bar Council may receive any grants, donations, gifts or benefactions for all or any of the purposes specified in sub-section (2) which shall be credited to be appropriate fund or funds constituted under that sub-section.

(a) Inserted by Act 60 of 1973, S. 6 (31.1.1974).

(b) Substituted for former S. 2, *ibid.*

7. Functions of Bar Council of India.— (1) The function of the Bar Council of India shall be—

(a) ****

(b) to lay down standards of professional conduct and etiquette for advocates;

(c) to lay down the procedure to be followed by its disciplinary committee and the disciplinary committee of each State Bar Council;

(d) to safeguard the rights, privileges and interests of advocates;

(e) to promote and support law reform;

(f) to deal with and dispose of any matter arising under this Act, which may be referred to it by a State Bar Council;

(g) to exercise general supervision and control over State Bar Councils;

(h) to promote legal education and to lay down standards of such education in consultation with the Universities in India imparting such education and the State Bar Councils;

(i) to recognise universities whose degree in law shall be qualification for enrolment as an advocate and for that purpose to visit and inspect Universities;

(ia) to conduct seminars and organise talks on legal topics by eminent jurists and publish journals and papers of legal interest;

(ib) to organise legal aid to the poor in the prescribed manner;

(ic) to recognise on a reciprocal basis foreign qualifications in law obtained outside India for the purpose of admission as an advocate under this Act;

(j) to manage and invest the funds of the Bar Council;

(k) to provide for the election of its members;

(l) to perform all other functions conferred on it by or under this Act;

(m) to do all other things necessary for discharging the aforesaid functions.

(2) The Bar Council of India may constitute one or more funds in the prescribed manner for the purpose of—

(a) giving financial assistance to organise welfare schemes for indigent, disabled or other advocates;

(b) giving legal aid or advice in accordance with the rules made in this behalf.

(3) The Bar Council of India may receive any grants, donations, gifts or benefactions for all or any of the purposes specified in sub-section (2) which shall be credited to the appropriate fund or funds constituted under the sub-section.

(a) S. 7 renumbered as sub-section (1) thereof, by Act 60 of 1973, S. 7 (31.1.1974) and clause (a) therein omitted.

(b) Inserted, *ibid.*

(c) Inserted, *ibid.*

7A. Membership in international bodies.—The Bar Council of India may become a member of international legal bodies such as the International Bar Association or the International Legal Aid Association, contribute such sums as it thinks fit to such bodies by way of subscription or otherwise and authorise expenditure on the participation of its representatives in any International legal conference or seminar.

(a) Inserted by Act 60 of 1973, S. 6 (31.1.1974).

8. Terms of office of members of State Bar Council.—(1) The term of office of an elected member of a State Bar Council [other than an elected member thereof referred to in Section 54 shall be five years] from the date of publication of the result of his election.

(2) An outgoing member shall continue in office until the publication of the result of the election of his successors.

(a) Substituted and deemed always to have been so, for the original section by Act 23 of 1966, S. 2.

(b) Substituted by Act 38 of 1977, S. 4 (31.10.77). Sub-section (2) of the said amending section runs as follows: "The amendment made by sub-section (1) to sub-section (1) of Section 8 of the principal Act shall apply also to an elected member of every State Bar Council who has not completed the term of four years at the commencement of this Act."

9. Disciplinary Committees.—(1) A Bar Council shall constitute one or more disciplinary committees, each of which shall consist of three persons of whom two shall be persons elected by the Council from amongst its members and the other shall be a person co-opted by the Council from amongst advocates who possess the qualifications specified in the proviso to sub-section (2) of Section 3 and who are not members of the Council, and the seniormost advocate amongst the members of a disciplinary committee shall be Chairman the thereof.

(2) Notwithstanding anything contained in sub-section (1), any disciplinary committee constituted prior to the commencement of the Advocates (Amendment) Act, 1964 may dispose of the proceedings pending before it as if this section had not been amended by the said Act.

(a) Substituted for original section by Act 21 of 1964, S. 5 (10.5.1964).

9A. Constitution of legal aid committees.—(1) A Bar Council may constitute one or more legal aid committees each of which shall consist of such number of members, not exceeding nine but not less than five, as may be prescribed.

(2) The qualifications, the method of selection and the term of office of the members of a legal aid committee shall be such as may be prescribed.

(a) Inserted by Act 80 of 1973, Sec. 9 (31.1.1974).

10. Constitution of committee other than disciplinary committees.—

(1) A State Bar Council shall constitute the following standing committees, namely:

(a) an executive committee consisting of five members elected by the Council from amongst its members;

(b) an enrolment committee consisting of three members elected by the Council from amongst its members.

(2) The Bar Council of India shall constitute the following standing committees, namely:

(a) an executive committee consisting of nine members elected by the Council from amongst its members.

(b) a legal education committee consisting of ten members, of whom members and five shall be persons co-opted by the Council who are not members thereof.

(3) A State Bar Council and the Bar Council of India may constitute from amongst its members such other committees as it may deem necessary for the purpose of carrying out the provisions of this Act.

10A. Transaction of business by Bar Councils and committees thereof.—

(1) The Bar Council of India shall meet at New Delhi.

(2) The Committees other than disciplinary committees constituted by the Bar Councils shall meet at the headquarters of the respective Bar Councils.

(3) Every Bar Council and every committee thereof except the disciplinary committees shall observe such rules of procedure in regard to the transaction of business at their meetings as may be prescribed.

(4) The disciplinary committees constituted under section 9 shall meet at such times and places and shall observe such rules of procedure in regard to the transaction of business at their meetings as may be prescribed.

(a) Inserted by Act 50 of 1973, Sec. 10 (31.1.1974).

10B. Disqualification of members of Bar Council.—An elected member of a Bar Council shall be deemed to have vacated his office if he is declared by the Bar Council of which he is a member to have been absent without sufficient excuse from three consecutive meetings of such Council, or if his name is, or any cause, removed from the roll of advocates or if he is otherwise disqualified under any rule made by the Bar Council of India.

(a) Original Sec. 10A renumbered as 10B by Act 60 of 1973, Sec. 10 (31.1.1974).

11. Staff of Bar Council.—(1) Every Bar Council shall appoint a secretary and may appoint an accountant and such number of other persons on its staff as it may deem necessary.

(2) The secretary and the accountant, if any, shall possess such qualifications as may be prescribed.

12. Accounts and audit.—(1) Every Bar Council shall cause to be maintained such books of accounts and other books in such form and in such manner as may be prescribed.

(2) The accounts of a Bar Council shall be audited by auditors duly qualified to act as auditors of companies under the Companies Act, 1956, at such times and in such manner as may be prescribed.

(3) As soon as may be practicable at the end of each financial years, but not later than the 31st day of December of the year next following, a State Bar Council shall send a copy of its accounts together with a copy of the report of the auditors thereon to the Bar Council of India and shall cause the same to be published in the Official Gazette.

(4) As soon as may be practicable at the end of each financial year, but not later than the 31st day of December of the year next following the Bar Council of India shall send a copy of its accounts together with a copy of the report of the auditors thereon to the Central Government and shall cause the same to be published in the Gazette of India.

(a) Substituted for former Sub-sections (3) and (4), by Act 60 of 1973, Sec. 11 (31.1.1974).

13. Vacancies in Bar Councils and committees thereof not to invalidate action taken.—No act done by a Bar Council or any committee thereof shall be called in question on the ground merely of the existence of any vacancy in, or any defect in the constitution of, the Council or committee, as the case may be.

14. Election to Bar Councils not to be questioned on certain grounds.— No election of a member to a Bar Council shall be called in question on the ground merely that due notice thereof has not been given to any person entitled to vote thereat, if notice of the date has, not less than thirty days before that date, been published in the Official Gazette.

15. Power to make rules.—(1) A Bar Council may make rules to carry out the purposes of this Chapter.

(2) In particular, and without prejudice to the generality of the foregoing power, such rules may provide for—

(a) the election of members of the Bar Council by secret ballot including the conditions subject to which persons can exercise the right to vote by postal ballot, the preparation and revision of electoral rolls and the manner in which the results of election shall be published;

(b) [Omitted];

(c) the manner of election of the Chairman and the Vice-Chairman of the Bar Council;

(d) the manner in which and the authority by which doubts and disputes as to the validity of an election to the Bar Council or to the office of' the Chairman or Vice-Chairman shall be finally decided;

(e) [Omitted];

(f) the filling of casual vacancies in the Bar Council;

(g) the powers and duties of the Chairman and the Vice-Chairman of the Bar Council;

(ga) the constitution of one or more funds by a Bar Council for the purpose of giving financial assistance or giving legal aid or advice referred to in sub-section (2) of Section 6 and sub-section (2) of section 7;

(gb) organisation of legal aid and advice to the poor, constitution and functions of committees and sub-committees for that purpose and description of proceedings in connection with which legal aid or advice may be given;

(h) the summing and holding of meetings of the Bar Council, the conduct of business thereat, and the number of members necessary to constitute a quorum;

(i) the constitution and functions of any committee of the Bar Council and the term of office of members of any such committee;

(j) the summoning and holding of meetings, the conduct of business of any such committee, and the number of members necessary to constitute a quorum;

(k) the qualifications and the conditions of service of the secretary, the accountant and other employees of the Bar Council;

(l) the maintenance of books of accounts and other books by the Bar Council;

(m) the appointment of auditors and the audit of the accounts of the Bar Council;

(n) the management and investment of the funds of the Bar Council.

(3) No rules made under this section by a State Bar Council shall have effect unless they have been approved by the Bar Council of India,

(a) Substituted by Act 60 of 1973, S. 6 (12.1.974).

(b) Omitted, *ibid.*

(c) Inserted by Act 38 of 1977, S. 5 (31.1.1974).

(d) Inserted, *ibid.*

(e) Omitted and deemed always to have been so by Act 23 of 1966, Sec. 3.

(f) Clauses (ga) and (gb) inserted by Act 60 of 1973, Sec. 12 (31.1.1974).

(g) Certain words omitted, *ibid.*

(h) Maharashtra:—For rules under S. 15, see Maha. Govt. Gaz. 4-4-1963, Pt. I (C.S.), p. 222; for rules under S. 15(2) (a) and (d), see Maha. Govt. Gaz., 5.12.1968, Pt. I (C.S.), p. 1164.

Andhra Pradesh:—For rules under Section 15, A.P. Gaz. 18.7.1963, Pt. II, R.S., p. 1029; and also A.P. Gaz., 6-12.1973, Pt. I (R.S.), p. 611.

Rajasthan:—For rules under S. 15(2) (a), (c), (d) and (f)—See Raj. Gaz. 30.11.1965, Pt. IV (Ga), p. 476.

Uttar Pradesh:—For rules under S. 15(2) (a), (c), (d), (e), (g) and (h)—See UP. Gaz. 26.10.1963, Pt. IA, p. 3264.

West Bengal:—For rules under S. 15(1) and 15(2) (a), (d), (f) and (k) and Section 15(2)(c) read with S. 8—See Cal. Gaz. 29.12.1963, Pt. I, pp. 2545, 2551 and 2550 respectively. For B.C. of W.B. Election Rules, 1973, See Cal. Gaz., 15.5.1975; Pt. I, p. 982.

CHAPTER III
ADMISSION AND ENROLMENT OF ADVOCATES

16. **Senior and other advocates.**—(1) There shall be two classes of advocates, namely, senior advocates and other advocates.

(2) An advocate may, with his consent, be designated as senior advocate if the Supreme Court or a High Court is of opinion that by virtue of his ability [standing at the Bar or special knowledge or experience in law] he is deserving of such distinction.

(3) Senior advocates shall, in the matter of their practice, be subject to such restrictions as the Bar Council of India may, in the interests of the legal profession, prescribe.

(4) An advocate of the Supreme Court who was a senior advocate of that Court immediately before the appointment day shall, for the purposes of this section, be deemed to be a senior advocate.

[Provided that where any such senior advocate makes an application before the 31st December, 1965 to the Bar Council maintaining the roll in which his name has been entered that he does not desire to continue as a senior advocate, the Bar Council may grant the application and the roll shall be altered accordingly].

(a) Chapter III was brought into force on 1.12.1961—Gaz. Ind., 1961, Extra, Pt. II, S. 3(ii), p. 1723.

(b) Substituted for certain words by Act 60 of 1973, S. 13 [31.1.1974].

(c) Added by Act 21 of 1964, S. 8 [16.5.1964].

17. **State Bar Council to maintain roll of advocates.**—(1) Every State Bar Council shall prepare and maintain a roll of advocates in which shall be entered the names and addresses of—

(a) all persons who were entered as advocates on the roll of any High Court under the Indian Bar Councils Act, 1926, immediately before the appointed day [including persons, being citizens of India, who before the 15th day of August, 1947, were enrolled as advocates under the said Act in any area which before the said date was comprised within India as defined in the Government of India Act, 1935 and who at any time] express an intention in the prescribed manner to practise within the jurisdiction of the Bar Council;

(b) all other persons who are admitted to be advocates on the roll of the State Bar Council under this Act on or after the appointed day.

(2) Each such roll of advocates shall consist of two parts, the first part containing the names of senior advocates and the second part, the names of other advocates.

(3) Entries in each part of the roll of advocates prepared and maintained by a State Bar Council under this section shall be in the order of seniority, [and, subject to any rule that may be made by Bar Council of India in this behalf, such seniority shall be determined] as follows:

(a) the seniority of an advocate referred to in clause (a) of sub-section (1) shall be determined in accordance with his date of enrolment under the Indian Bar Councils Act, 1926;

(b) the seniority of any person who was a senior advocate of the Supreme Court immediately before the appointed day shall, for the purposes of the first part of the State roll, be determined in accordance with such principles as the Bar Council of India may specify;

(c) Omitted;

(d) the seniority of any other person who, on or after the appointed day, is enrolled as a senior advocate or is admitted as an advocate shall be determined by the date of such enrolment or admission, as the case may be.

(4) No person shall be enrolled as an advocate on the roll of more than one State Bar Council.

(a) Substituted for the words "within the prescribed time" by Act 60 of 1973, S. 14 (31.1.1974).

(b) Substituted for the words "and, such seniority shall be determined" by Act 21 of 1964, S. 9 (16.5.1964).

(c) Omitted by Act 60 of 1973, S. 14 (31.1.1974).

(d) In respect of the Bar Council of H.P. and the Bar Council of Assam, Nagaland, Meghalaya, Manipur and Tripura provisions of this section shall apply subject to the modifications given below:

(4)(1). The provisions of Section 17 of the Advocates Act shall have effect in respect of the roll of the Bar Council of Himachal Pradesh subject to the modifications that—(a) for clause (a) of sub-section (1) of the said section 17, the following clause shall be substituted, namely:

"(a) all persons who were entered as advocates on the roll of the Bar Council of Punjab and Haryana immediately before the day appointed under clause (b) of Section 2 of the State of Himachal Pradesh Act, 1970, and who within three months from that day express in such manner as the Bar Council of India may, by rules, prescribe an intention in writing to practise within the jurisdiction of the Bar Council of Himachal Pradesh; (b) in clause (a) of sub-section (3) of the said section 17, for the words and figures "with his date of enrolment under the Indian Bar Councils Act, 1926," the words "with his seniority on the roll of the Bar Council of Punjab and Haryana" shall be substituted.

(5) Notwithstanding anything contained in the Advocates Act as amended or modified by sub-sections (3) and (4).

(a) in the case of the first Bar Council of Himachal Pradesh under that Act, the fifteen members required to be elected under clause (b) of sub-section (2) of Section (3) of that Act, as amended by sub-section (3), shall be nominated by the Chief Justice of the High Court of Himachal Pradesh from amongst advocates who are entitled as or right to practise in the High Court of Himachal Pradesh and are ordinarily practising within the territories comprised in the State of Himachal Pradesh and the term of office of the members so nominated shall be one year from the date of the first meeting of the Council or until successors are duly elected in accordance with the provisions of the said Act, whichever is earlier;

(b) until the members of the first Bar Council of Himachal Pradesh required to be nominated under clause (a) are duly nominated in accordance with the provisions of that clause, the Bar Council of Punjab and Haryana shall function as the Bar Council of Himachal Pradesh and the provisions of the Advocates Act shall, so far as may be, apply accordingly;

(c) the names of persons entered on the roll of the Bar Council of Himachal Pradesh in accordance with the provisions of clause (a) of sub-section (1) of Section 17 of the Advocates Act as modified by sub-section (4), shall, as from the date or dates on which the names are so entered, stand removed from the roll of the Bar Council of Punjab and Haryana;

(d) any proceedings which may be pending or which may be instituted against any person before or by the Bar Council of Punjab and Haryana immediately before his name is removed under clause (c) from the roll of that Bar Council may after such removal be continued or instituted before or by the Bar Council of Himachal Pradesh;

(e) every person who immediately before his name stands removed from the roll of the Bar Council of Punjab and Haryana in accordance with the provisions of clause (c) is a member of the

Bar Council as from the date on which his name stands so removed from the roll of that Bar Council;

(f) the rules made or deemed to have been made by the Bar Council of Punjab and Haryana and in force immediately before the date on which the first Bar Council of Himachal Pradesh is duly constituted in accordance with the provisions of clause (a) shall, subject to such modifications and adaptations as may be made therein by the Chairman of the Bar Council of Himachal Pradesh, be deemed to be rules made by the Bar Council of Himachal Pradesh and shall have effect accordingly.

(6) As soon as may be after the first Bar Council of Himachal Pradesh is duly constituted in accordance with the provisions of clause (a) of sub-section (5), the assets and liabilities of the Bar Council of Punjab and Haryana shall be apportioned between that Bar Council of and the Bar Council of Himachal Pradesh in such manner and proportion as may be agreed upon by the two Bar Councils and in default of agreement with reference to any matter, the matter shall be referred to the Chairman of the Bar Council of India and his decision thereon shall be final.

(a) For clause (a) of sub-section (1) of the said section 17, the following clause shall be substituted, namely:

(a) all persons who were entered as advocates:

(i) On the roll of the Bar Council of Assam and Nagaland immediately before the day appointed under clause (b) of Section 2 of the North-Eastern Areas (Reorganisation) Act, 1971;

(ii) On the roll of the Bar Council of West Bengal immediately before that day and who, within three months from that day, express in such manner as the Bar Council of India may, by rules, prescribe their intention in writing to practise within the jurisdiction of the Bar Council of Assam, Nagaland, Meghalaya, Manipur and Tripura;

(b) in clause (a) of sub-section (3) of the said Section 17, for the words and figures "with his date of enrolment under the Indian Bar Councils Act, 1926," the words "with his seniority on the roll of the Bar Council of Assam and Nagaland or, as the case may be, the Bar Council of West Bengal" shall be substituted.

(7) Notwithstanding anything contained in the Advocates Act, as amended or modified by sub-sections (3) and (4),—

(a) In the case of first Bar Council of Assam, Nagaland, Meghalaya, Manipur and Tripura under that Act, the fifteen members required to be elected under clause (b) of sub-section (2) of Section 3 of that Act, shall be nominated by the Chief Justice of the common High Court from amongst the advocates who are entitled as of right to practise in that High Court and are ordinarily practising within the territories comprised in the States of Assam, Manipur, Meghalaya, Nagaland and Tripura and the Union territories of Mizoram and Arunachal Pradesh and the term of office of the members so nominated shall be one year from the date of the first meeting of the Council or until their successors are duly elected in accordance with the provisions of the said Act, whichever is earlier;

(b) the names of persons entered on the roll of the Bar Council of Assam, Nagaland, Meghalaya, Manipur and Tripura from the roll of the Bar Council of West Bengal in accordance with the provisions of clause (a) of sub-section (1) of Section 17 of the Advocates Act, as modified by sub-section (4), shall, as from the date or dates on which the names are so entered, stand removed from the roll of the Bar Council of West Bengal;

(c) any proceedings which were pending or which may be instituted against any person before or by the Bar Council of Assam and Nagaland or by the Bar Council of West Bengal immediately before his name is entered in the roll of the Bar Council of Assam, Nagaland, Meghalaya, Manipur and Tripura in accordance with the provisions of clause (a) of sub-section (1) of Section 17 of the Advocates Act, as modified by sub-section (4), may, after such entry, be continued or instituted before or by the Bar Council of Assam, Nagaland, Meghalaya, Manipur and Tripura;

(d) every person who, immediately before his name stands removed from the roll of the Bar Council of West Bengal in accordance with the provisions of clause (b), is a member of the Bar Council of West Bengal, shall cease to be a member of that Council as from the date on which his name stands so removed from the roll of that Bar Council;

(e) the rules made or deemed to have been made by the Bar Council of Assam and Nagaland and in force immediately before the date on which the first Bar Council of Assam, Nagaland, Meghalaya, Manipur and Tripura is duly constituted in accordance with the provisions of clause (a), shall, subject to such modifications and adaptations as may be made therein by the Chairman of the Bar Council of Assam, Nagaland, Meghalaya, Manipur and Tripura, be deemed to be rules made by that Bar Council and shall have effect accordingly.

(8)(a) As from the appointed day, the assets and liabilities of the Bar Council of Assam and Nagaland shall pass to the Bar Council of Assam, Nagaland, Meghalaya, Manipur and Tripura.

(b) The assets and liabilities of the Bar Council of West Bengal shall be apportioned between that Bar Council and the Bar Council of Assam, Nagaland, Meghalaya, Manipur and Tripura in such manner and proportion as may be agreed upon by the Bar Councils and in default of agreement with reference to any matter, the matter shall be referred to the Chairman of the Bar Council of India and his decision thereon shall be final.

Explanation.—Expressions used in this section but not defined in this Act shall have the meanings assigned to them respectively in the Advocates Act.—See Act 81 of 1971, S. 34 (4), (5) and (6).

18. Transfer of name from one State roll to another.—(1) Notwithstanding anything contained in Section 17, any person whose name is entered as an advocate on the roll of any State Bar Council may make an application in the prescribed from to the Bar Council of India for the transfer of his name from the roll of that State Bar Council to the roll of any other State Bar Council and, on receipt of any such application the Bar Council of India shall direct that the name of such person shall, without the payment of any fee, be removed from the roll of the first mentioned State Bar Council and entered in the roll of the other State Bar Council and the State Bar Councils concerned shall comply with such direction:

[Provided that where any such application for transfer is made by a person against whom any disciplinary proceeding is pending or where for any other reason it appears to the Bar Council of India that the application for transfer has not been made *bonafide* and that the transfer should not be made, the Bar Council of India may, after giving the person making the application an opportunity of making a representation in this behalf, reject the application],

(2) For the removal of doubts, it is hereby declared that where on an application made by an advocate under sub-section (1), his name is transferred from the roll of one State Bar Council to that of another, he shall retain the same seniority in the latter roll to which he was entitled in the former roll.

(a) Proviso added by Act 21 of 1964, S. 10 (16.5.1964).

(Note: "The Committee are of the opinion that although an advocate is not permitted to enrol himself on the roll of more than one State Bar Council, he should have the right to get his name transferred from one State roll to another if he so chooses on account of his changing the venue of his practice or for some other reason." J.C.R.).

19. State Bar Councils to send copies of rolls of advocates to the Bar Council of India.—Every State Bar Council shall send to the Bar Council of India an authenticated copy of the roll of advocates prepared by it for the first time under this Act and shall thereafter, communicate to the Bar Council of India all alterations in, and addition to, any such roll, as soon as the same have been made.

20. Special provision for enrolment of certain Supreme Court advocates.—(1) Notwithstanding anything contained in this Chapter, every advocate who was entitled as of right to practise in the Supreme Court immediately before the appointed day whose name is not entered in any State roll may, within the prescribed time, express his intention in the provision of clauses. (a), (b), (e) and (f) of sub-section (1).

(2) Notwithstanding anything contained in sub-section (1) a person who—

(a) has, for at least three years, been a vakil or a pleader or a mukhtar, or was entitled at any time to be enrolled under any law as an advocate or a High Court (including a High Court of a former Part B State) or of a Court of Judicial Commissioner in any Union Territory; or

(aa) before the 1st day of December, 1962 was entitled otherwise than as an advocate to practise the profession of law [whether by way of pleading or acting or both) by virtue of the provisions of any law, or who would have been so entitled had he not been in public service on the said date; or]

(b) Omitted;

(c) before the 1st day of April, 1937, has been an advocate of any High Court in any area which was comprised within Burma as defined in the Government of India Act, 1935; or

(d) is entitled to be enrolled as an advocate under any rule made by the Bar Council of India in this behalf; may be admitted as an advocate on a State roll if he—

(i) makes an application for such enrolment in accordance with the provisions of this Act; and

(ii) fulfils the conditions specified in clauses (a), (b), (e) and (f) of sub-section (1).

(3) Omitted.

(a) For Rules made by the Goa, Daman and Diu Judicial Commissioner's Court for registration of outside advocate under S. 14(1) of Regn. 10 of 1963, see Goa, Gaz., 25.6.1964, p. 167.

(b) Substituted for the words 28th day of February 1963 by Act 60 of 1973, S. 18(I) (31.1.1974).

(c) Substituted for former clause (iii), *ibid.*, S. 18 (II) (31.1.74).

(d) Substituted for the words 'he is a barrier', *ibid.*, S. 18(III) (31.1.1974).

(e) Inserted by Act 107 of 1976, S. 6 (15.10.1976).

(f) Omitted by Act 60 of 1973, S. 18(III) (31.1.74).

(g) Substituted, *ibid.*

(h) Inserted by Act 14 of 1962, S. 2 (30.3.1962).

(i) Substituted for original words by Act 21 of 1964, S. 13B (16.5.1964).

(j) Sub-sections (3) and (4) inserted, *ibid.*, S. 13C (16.5.1964).

(k) Words "before the 31st day of March 1964" and 'then in force' omitted by Act 33 of 1968, S. 2 (w.e.f. 5.6.1974).

(l) Inserted by Act 60 of 1973, S. 18(III) (31.1.1964).

(m) Omitted, *ibid.*

(n) Sub-section (4) omitted by Act 107 of 1976, S. 6(ii) (15.10.76).

24A. Disqualification for enrolment.—(1) No person shall be admitted as an advocate on a State roll—

(a) if he is convicted of an offence involving moral turpitude;

(b) if he is convicted of an offence under the provisions of the Untouchability (Offences) Act, 1955;

Provided that the disqualification for enrolment as aforesaid shall cease to have effect after a period of two years has elapsed since his release.

(2) Nothing contained in sub-section (1) shall apply to a person who having been found guilty is dealt with under the provisions of the Probation of Offenders Act, 1958].

(a) Inserted by Act 60 of 1973, S. 19 (31.1.1974).

25. Authority to whom applications for enrolment may be made.—An application for admission as an advocate shall be made in the prescribed form to the State Bar Council within whose jurisdiction the applicant proposes to practise.

26. Disposal of applications for admission as an advocate.—(1) A State Bar Council shall refer every application for admission as an advocate to its enrolment committee, and subject to the provisions of sub-sections (2) and (3) [and to any direction that may be given in writing by the State Bar Council in this behalf] such committee shall dispose of the application in the prescribed manner:

Provided that the Bar Council of India may, if satisfied, either on a reference made to it in this behalf or otherwise, that any person has got his name entered on the roll of advocates by misrepresentation as to an essential fact or by fraud or undue influence, remove the name of such person from the roll of advocates after giving him an opportunity of being heard].

(2) Where the enrolment committee of a State Bar Council proposes to refuse any such application, it shall refer the application for opinion to the Bar Council of India and every such reference shall be accompanied by a statement of the grounds in support of the refusal of the application.

(3) The enrolment committee of a State Bar Council shall dispose of any application referred to the Bar Council of India under sub-section (2) in conformity with the opinion of the Bar Council of India.

(4) Where the enrolment committee of a State Bar Council has refused any application for admission as an advocate on its roll, the State Bar Council shall, as soon as may be, send intimation to all other State Bar Councils about such refusal stating the name, address and qualifications of the person whose application was refused and the grounds for the refusal.

(a) Inserted by Act 21 of 1964, S. 14(a) (16.5.64).

(b) Added, *ibid.*, S. 14(b) (16.5.64).

(c) Inserted, *ibid.*, S. 14(c) (16.5.64).

26A. Power to remove names from roll.—A State Bar Council may remove from the State roll the name of any advocate who is dead or from whom a request has been received to that effect.

(a) Substituted by Act 60 of 1973, S. 20 (31.1.1974).

27. Application once refused not to be entertained by another Bar Council except in certain circumstances.—Where a State Bar Council has refused application of any person for admission as an advocate on its roll, no other State Bar Council shall entertain an application for admission of such person as an advocate on its roll, except with the previous consent in writing of the State Bar Council which refused the application and of the Bar Council of India.

28. Power to make rules.—(1) A State Bar Council may make rules to carry out the purposes of this Chapter.

(2) In particular, and without prejudice to the generality of the foregoing power, such rules may provide for—

(a) the time within which and form in which an advocate shall express his intention for the entry of his name in the roll of a State Bar Council under Section 20;

(b) (omitted);

(c) the form in which an application shall be made to the Bar Council for admission as an advocate on its roll and the manner in which such application shall be disposed of by the enrolment committed of the Bar Council;

(d) the conditions subject to which a person may be admitted as an advocate on any such roll;

(e) the instalments in which the enrolment fee may be paid.

(3) No rules made under this Chapter shall have effect unless they have been approved by the Bar Council of India.

(a) Substituted for original clause (a) by Act 60 of 1973, S. 21 (31.1.1974).

(b) Omitted by Act 60 of 1973, S. 21 (31.1.1974).

(c) For Rules made under Clauses (a), (b), (c) and (d) in Punjab—See Punjab Govt. Gaz. 29-3-1963, Pt. III, p. 359. These rules until repealed or modified would also be applicable in Haryana State, and Union Territory of Chandigarh.

For rules framed under Clauses 2 (b) and (d) in Rajasthan, see Raj. Gaz., 30.9.65, Pt. IV (ga), p. 311 (83).

For rules framed under CI. 2(b) in Uttar Pradesh, see U.P Gaz., 2.9.1967, Pt. IA.

For rules framed under the Section in Andhra Pradesh, see A.P. Gaz., 13.12.1973, Pt. II (R.S.), p. 611.

CHAPTER IV
RIGHT TO PRACTISE

29. Advocates to be the only recognised class of persons entitled to practise law.—Subject to the provisions of this Act and any rules made thereunder, there shall, as from the appointed day, be only one class of persons entitled to practise the profession of law, namely, advocates.

(a) Section enforced on from 1-6-1969—See Gaz. of Ind., 1969, Pt. II, S. 3(ii), Ext., p. 569.

30. Right of advocates to practise.—Subject to the provisions of this Act, every Advocate whose name is entered in the [State roll] shall be entitled as of right to practise throughout the territories to which this Act extends,

(i) in all courts including the Supreme Court;

(ii) before any tribunal or person legally authorised to take evidence; and

(iii) before any other authority or person before whom such advocate is by or under any law for the time being in force entitled to practise.

(a) See however the following provision in the Laccadive, Minicoy and Amindivi Islands (Civil Courts) Regulation, 1965 (9 of 1965), S. 20 (c):

"(c) no appearance, application or act in or to the Court, required or authorised by law to be made or done by a party in such a Court, required or authorised by law to be made or done by a party in such a Court, shall be made or done by a pleader (as defined in the Code of Civil Procedure, 1908) save with the permission of Court;"

(b) Submitted for the words "Common roll" by Act 60 of 1973, S. 22 (31-1-1974).

31. Special provision for attorney.—Omitted by Act 107 of 1976, Sec. 7 (1-1-1977).

32. Power of Court to permit appearances in particular cases.—Notwithstanding anything contained in this Chapter, any court, authority or person may permit any person, not enrolled as an advocate under this Act to appear before it or him in any particular case.

(a) This section was brought into force on 4th January 1963, see Gaz. of India 4-1-1963, Pt. II, Sec. 3(ii), p. 1.

33. Advocates alone entitled to practise.—Except as otherwise provided in this Act or in any other law for the time being in force, no person shall on or after the appointed day, be entitled to practise in any court or before any authority or persons unless he is enrolled as an advocate under this Act.

(a) Section enforced on and from 1-6-1969.

34. Power of High Courts to make rules.—(1) The High Court may make rules laying down the conditions subject to which an advocate shall be permitted to practise in the High Court and the courts subordinate thereto.

(1A) The High Court shall make rules for fixing and regulating by taxation or otherwise the fees payable as costs by any party in respect of the fees of his adversary's advocate upon all proceedings in the High Court or in any Court subordinate thereto.

(2) Without prejudice to the provisions contained in sub-section (1), the High Court at Calcutta may make rules providing for the holding of the Intermediated and the Final examinations for articled clerks to be passed by the persons referred to in Section 58AG for the purpose of being admitted as advocates on the State roll and any other matter connected therewith.

(3) Omitted.

(a) For rules framed under S. 34(1) in Bihar and Madhya Pradesh, see Bih. Gaz., 1-5-1968, Pt. II, p. 1006 and M.P. Gaz., 23-8-1961, Pt. IV (ga), p. 697; in Orissa, see On. Gaz., 10-10-69, Pt. III, p. 953; for rules in Rajasthan, see Raj. Gaz., 12-2-197A, Pt. IV (Gass) (i), p. 249; in Punjab, see Punj. Gaz., 27-3-1970 Pt. III (L.S.), p. 143; in Tamil Nadu, see Ft. St. George Gaz., 21-1-1970, Pt. V, p. 74; in W.B., see Cal. Gaz., 11-12-1969, Pt. I, p. 2124; in U.P., see U.P. Gaz., 14-6-69, Pt. HI, p. 113; in Kerala, see Kerala Gaz., 23-9-1964, Pt. III, No. 37, (G. 3008); for Rules framed by Gauhati High Court, see Tripura Gaz. 13-10-72, Ext. (No. 137.)

(b) Sub-section (1A) inserted by Act 60 of 1973, S. 23 (31-1-1974).

(c) Sub-section (2) inserted by Act 38 of 1977, S. 6 (w.e.f. 31-10-77).

(d) Omitted by Act 107 of 1976, S. 8 (1-1-1977). Sub-sections (2) and (3) were both omitted by this provision). Original section was enforced on and from 1-6-1969.

CHAPTER V
CONDUCT OF ADVOCATES

35. **Punishment of Advocates for misconduct.**—(1) Where on receipt of a complaint or otherwise a State Bar Council has reason to believe that any advocate on its roll has been guilty of professional or other misconduct, it shall refer the case for disposal to its disciplinary committee.

(1A) The State Bar Council may, either of its own motion or on application made to it by any person interested, withdraw a proceeding pending before its disciplinary committee and direct the inquiry to be made by any other disciplinary committee of that State Bar Council.

(2) The disciplinary committee of a State Bar Council shall fix a date for the hearing of the case and shall cause a notice thereof to be given to the advocate concerned and to the Advocate General of the State,

(3) The disciplinary committee of a State Bar Council after giving the advocate concerned and the Advocate-General an opportunity of being heard, may make any of the following orders, namely:

(a) dismiss the complaint or, where the proceedings were initiated at the instance of the State Bar Council, direct that the proceedings be field;

(b) reprimand the advocate;

(c) suspend the advocate from practice for such period as it may deem fit;

(d) remove the name of the advocate from the State roll of advocates.

(4) Where an advocate is suspended from practice under clause (c) of sub-section (3), he shall, during the period of suspension, be debarred from practising in any Court or before any authority or person in India.

(5) Where any notice is issued to the Advocate-General may appear before the disciplinary committee of the State Bar Council either in person or through any advocate appearing on his behalf.

[*Explanation.*—In this section, [Section 37 and Section 38] the expressions "Advocate-General and "Advocate-General of the State" shall, in relation to the Union territory of Delhi, mean the Additional Solicitor General of India.]

(a) Chapter V was brought into force on 1st September, 1963—see Gaz. of India, 1963, Pt II, Sec. 3(ii), p. 513.

(b) Inserted by Act 21 of 1964, S. 17 [16-5-1964].

(c) Sub-section (1A) inserted by Act 60 of 1973, S. 24 [31-1-1974].

(d) Words "if it does not summarily reject the complaint" omitted, *ibid.*

(e) Inserted after the words "In this section", *ibid.*

36. Disciplinary powers of Bar Council of India.—(1) Where on receipt of a complaint or otherwise the Bar Council of India has reason to believe that any advocate whose name is not entered on any State roll has been guilty of professional or other misconduct, it shall refer the case for disposal to its disciplinary committee.

(2) Notwithstanding anything contained in this Chapter, the disciplinary committee of the Bar Council of India may, [either of its own motion or on a report by any State Bar Council or on any application made to it by any person interested] withdraw for inquiry before itself any proceedings for disciplinary action against any advocate pending before the disciplinary committee of any State Bar Council and dispose of the same.

(3) The disciplinary committee of the Bar Council of India, in disposing of any case under this section, shall observe, so far as may be, the procedure laid down in Section 35, the references to the Advocate-General in that section being construed as references to the Attorney-General of India.

(4) In disposing of any proceedings under this section the disciplinary committee of the Bar Council of India may make any order which the disciplinary committee of a State Bar Council can make under sub-section (3) of Section 35, and where any proceedings have been withdrawn for inquiry [before the disciplinary committee of the Bar Council of India], the State Bar Council concerned shall give effect to any such order.

(a) Certain words omitted by Act 60 of 1973, S. 25 [31-1-1974].

(b) Substituted for certain words, *ibid.*

36A. Changes in constitution of disciplinary committees.—Whenever in respect of any proceedings under Section 35 or Section 36 a disciplinary committee of the State Bar Council or a disciplinary committee of the Bar Council of India ceases to exercise jurisdiction and is succeeded by another committee which has and exercise jurisdiction and is succeeded by another committee which has and exercises jurisdiction, the disciplinary committee of the State Bar Council or the disciplinary committee or the Bar Council or the disciplinary committee of the Bar Council of India, as the case may be, so succeeding may continue the proceedings from the stage at which the proceedings were so left by its predecessor committee.

36B. Disposal of disciplinary proceedings.—(1) The disciplinary committee of a State Bar Council shall dispose of the complaint received by it under Section 35 expeditiously and in each case the proceedings shall be concluded within a period of one year from the date of the receipt of the complaint or the date of initiation of the proceedings at the instance of the State Bar Council, as the case may be, failing which such proceedings shall stand transferred to the Bar Council of India which may dispose of the same as if it were a proceeding withdrawn for inquiry under sub-section (2) of Section 36.

(2) Notwithstanding anything contained in sub-section (1), where on the commencement of the Advocates (Amendment) Act, 1973, any proceedings in respect of any disciplinary matter against an advocate is pending before the disciplinary committee of a State Bar Council, that disciplinary committee of the State Bar Council shall dispose of the same within a period of six months from the date of such commencement or within a period of one year from the date of the receipt of the complaint or, as the case may be, the date of initiation of the proceedings at the instance the State Bar Council, whichever is later, failing which such proceedings shall stand transferred to the Bar Council, whichever is later, failing which such proceedings shall stand transferred to the Bar Council of India, for disposal under sub-section (1).

37. Appeal to the Bar Council of India.—(1) Any person aggrieved by an order of the disciplinary committee of a State Bar Council made under Section 35) [or an Advocate-General of the State] may, within sixty days of the date of the communication of the order to him, prefer an appeal to the Bar Council of India which may pass such order [including an order varying the punishment awarded by the disciplinary committee of the State Bar Council] thereon as it deems fit:

Provided that no order of the disciplinary committee of the State Bar Council shall be varied by the disciplinary committee of the Bar Council of India so as to prejudicially affect the person aggrieved without giving him reasonable opportunity of being heard.

(a) Substituted for the words "under sub-section (3) of Section 35" by Act 21 of 1964, S. 18 [16-5-1964].

(b) Certain words in sub-sections (1) and (2), and the proviso, inserted by Act 60 of 1973, S. 27 [31-1-1974].

38. Appeal to the Supreme Court.—Any person aggrieved by an order made by the disciplinary committee of the Bar Council of India under Section 36 [or the Attorney-General of India or the Advocate-General of the State concerned, as the case may be,] may within sixty days of the date on which the order is communicated to him prefer an appeal to the Supreme Court and the Supreme Court may pass such order [including an order varying the punishment awarded by the disciplinary committee of the Bar Council of India] thereon as it deems fit:

Provided that no order of the disciplinary committee of the Bar Council of India shall be varied by the Supreme Court so as to prejudicially affect the person aggrieved without giving him a reasonable opportunity of being heard.

(a) Certain words in the main provision, and the proviso, inserted by Act 60 of 1973, Section 28 (31-1-1974).

39. Application of Sections 5 and 12 of Limitation Act, 1963.—The provisions of Sections 5 and 12 of the Limitation Act, 1963, shall, so far as may be apply to appeals under Section 37 and Section 38.

40. Stay of order.—(1) An appeal, made under Section 37 or Section 38, shall not operate as a stay of the order appealed against, but the disciplinary committee of the Bar Council of India, or the Supreme Court, as the case may be, may, for sufficient cause, direct the stay of such order on such terms and conditions as it may deem fit.

(2) Where an application is made for stay of the order before the expiration of the time allowed for appealing therefrom under Section 37 or Section 38, the disciplinary committee of the State Bar Council, or the disciplinary committee of the Bar Council of India as the case may be, may, for sufficient cause, direct the stay of such order or such terms and conditions as it may deem fit.

(a) Original S. 40 renumbered as sub-section (1) thereof by Act 60 of 1973, S. 30 [31-1-1974].

(b) Sub-section (2) inserted thereafter, *ibid.*

41. Alteration in roll of advocates.—(1) Where an order is made under this Chapter reprimanding or suspending an advocate, a record of the punishment shall be entered against his name:

(a) in the case of an advocate whose name is entered in a State roll, in that roll;

(b) (Omitted); and where any order is made removing an advocate from practice, his name shall be struck off the State roll.

(2) (Omitted);

(3) Where any advocate is suspended or removed from practice, the certificate granted to him under Section 22, in respect of his enrolment shall be recalled.

(a) Clause (b) and sub-section (2), and certain words in sub-section (1) omitted by Act 60 of 1973, S. 31 [31-1-1974].

42. Powers of disciplinary committee.—(1) The disciplinary committee of a Bar Council shall have the same powers as are vested in a Civil Court under the Code of Civil Procedure, 1908, in respect of the following matters, namely:

(a) summoning and enforcing the attendance of any person and examining him on oath;

(b) requiring discovery and production of any documents;

(c) receiving evidence on affidavits;

(d) requisitioning any public record or copies thereof from any Court or office;

(e) issuing commission for the examination of witnesses or documents;

(f) any other matter which may be prescribed:

Provided that no such disciplinary committee shall have the right to require the attendance of:

(a) any presiding officer of a Court except with the previous sanction of the High Court to which such Court is subordinate;

(b) any officer of a revenue Court except with the previous sanction of the State Government.

(2) All proceedings before a disciplinary committee of a Bar Council shall be deemed to be judicial proceedings within the meaning of Sections 193 and 228 of the Indian Penal Code, and every such disciplinary committee shall be deemed to be a Civil Court for the purposes of Sections 480, 482 and 485 of the Code of Criminal Procedure, 1898.

(3) For the purposes of exercising any of the powers conferred by sub-section (1), a disciplinary committee may send to any Civil Court in the territories to which this Act extends, any summons or other process, for the attendance of a witness or the production of a document required by the committee or any commission which it desires to issue, and the Civil Court committee or any commission which it desires to issue, and the Civil Court shall cause such process to be served or such

commission to be issued, as the case may be, and may enforce any such process as if it were a process for attendance or production before itself.

(4) Notwithstanding the absence of the Chairman or any member of a disciplinary committee on a date fixed for the hearing of a case before it, the disciplinary committee may if it so thinks fit, hold or continue the proceedings on the date so fixed and no such proceedings and no order made by the disciplinary committee in any such proceedings shall be invalid merely by reason of the absence of the Chairman or member thereof on any such date:

Provided that no final orders of the nature referred to in sub-section (3) of Section 35 shall be made in any proceeding unless the Chairman and other members of the disciplinary committee are present.

(5) Where no final orders of the nature referred to in sub-section 35 can be made in any proceedings in accordance with the opinion of the Chairman and the members of a disciplinary committee either for want of majority opinion amongst themselves or otherwise, the case with their opinion thereon, shall be laid before the Chairman of the Bar Council concerned or if the Chairman of the Bar Council is acting as the Chairman of the Bar member or the disciplinary committee before the Vice-Chairman of the Bar Council, and the said Chairman or the Vice-Chairman of the Bar Council, as the case may be, after such hearing as he thinks fit, shall deliver his opinion and the final order of the disciplinary committee shall follow such opinion.

(a) Sub-sections (4) and (5) inserted by Act 60 of 1973, S. 32 [31-1-1974].

42A. Powers of Bar Council of India and other committees.—The provisions of Section 42 shall so far as may be, apply in relation to the Bar Council of India, the enrolment committee, the election committee, the legal aid committee, or any other committee of a Bar Council as they apply in relation to the disciplinary committee of a Bar Council:

(a) Inserted by Act 60 of 1973, S. 33 (31-1-1974).

43. Cost of proceedings before a disciplinary committee.—The disciplinary committee of a Bar Council may make such order as to the cost of any proceedings before it as it may deem fit and any such order shall be executable as if it were an order—

(a) in the case of an order of the disciplinary committee of the Bar Council of India, of the Supreme Court;

(b) in the case of an order of the disciplinary committee of a State Bar Council, of the High Court.

44. **Review of orders of disciplinary committee.**—The disciplinary committee of a Bar Council may of its own motion or otherwise review any order [within sixty days of the date of that order] passed by it under this chapter:

Provided that so order of review of the disciplinary committee of a State Bar Council shall have effect unless it has been approved by the Bar Council of India.

(a) Inserted by Act 60 of 1973, S. 34, (31-1-1974).

CHAPTER VI
MISCELLANEOUS

45. Penalty for person illegally practising in Courts and before other authorities.—Any person who practises in any Court or before any authority or person, in nor before whom he is not entitled to prartise under the provisions of this Act shall be punishable with imprisonment for a term which may extend to, six months.

(a) For the enforcement of this chapter see note under S. 1.

46. Payment of part of enrolment fees to the Bar Council of India.— Every State Bar Council shall, for each financial year commencing on or after the 1st day of April, 1976, pay to the Bar Council of India **a** sum equivalent to twenty per cent of the total of the enrolment fees realised by it under this Act during that year, before the thirtieth day of April of the succeeding financial year.]

(a) Original section 46 substituted by Act 107 of 1976, S. 9 (15.10.1976).

46A. Financial assistance to State Bar Council.—The Bar Council of India may if it is satisfied that any State Bar Council is in need of funds for the purpose of performing its functions under this Act, give such financial assistance as it deems fit to that Bar Council by way of grant or otherwise.

(a) Inserted by Act of 1973, S. 35 [31.1.1974].

47. Reciprocity.—(1) Where any country, specified by the Central Government in this behalf by notification in the Office Gazette, prevents citizens of India from practising the profession of law or subjects them to unfair discrimination in that country, no subject of any such country shall be entitled to practise the profession of law in India.

(2) Subject to the provisions of sub-section (1), the Bar Council of India may prescribe the conditions, if any, subject to which foreign qualifications in law obtained by persons other than citizens of India shall be recognised for the purpose of admission as an advocate under this Act.

48. Indemnity against legal proceedings.—No suit or other legal proceedings shall lie against any Bar Council or any committee thereof or a member of a Bar Council [or any committee thereof] for any act in good faith done or intended to be done in pursuance of the provisions of this Act or of any rule made thereunder.

48A. Power of revision.—(1) The Bar Council of India may, at any time, call for the record of any proceeding under this Act which has been disposed of by a State Bar Council or a Committee thereof, and from which no appeal lies, for the purpose of satisfying itself as to the legality or propriety of such disposal and may pass such orders in relation thereto as it may think fit.

(2) No order which prejudicially affects any person shall be passed under this section without giving him a reasonable opportunity of being heard.

(a) Inserted by Act 21 of 1964, S. 19 [16.5.1964].

48AA. Review.—The Bar Council of India or any of its committees, other than its disciplinary committee, may of its own motion or otherwise review any order, within sixty days of the date of that order, passed by it under this Act.

(a) Inserted by Act 21 of 1964, S. 19 [16.5.1964].

48B. Power to give directions.—(1) For the proper and efficient discharge of the functions of a State Bar Council or any Committee thereof, the Bar Council of India may, in the exercise of its powers of general supervision and control give such directions to the State Bar Council or any committee thereof as may appear to it to be necessary, and the State Bar Council or any Committee thereof as may appear to it to be necessary, and the State Bar Council or the Committee shall comply with such directions.

(2) Where a State Bar Council is unable to perform its functions for any reason whatsoever, the Bar Council of India may, without prejudice to the generality of the foregoing power, give such directions to the ex-officio member thereof as may appear to it to be necessary, and such directions shall have effect, notwithstanding anything contained in the rules, made by the State Bar Council.

(a) Inserted by Act 21 of 1964, S. 19 [16.5.1964].

49. General power of the Bar Council of India to make rules.—(1) The Bar Council of India may make rules for discharging its functions under this Act, and, in particular, such rules may prescribe—

(a) the conditions subject to which an advocate may be entitled to vote at an election to the State Bar Council including the qualifications or disqualifications of voters, and the manner in which an electoral roll of voters may be prepared and reviewed by a State Bar Council;

(ab) qualifications for membership of a Bar Council and the disqualifications for such membership;

(ac) the time within which and the manner in which effect may be given to the proviso to sub-section (2) of Section 3;

(ad) the manner in which the name of any advocate may be prevented from being entered in more than one State roll;

(ae) the manner in which the seniority among advocates may be determined;

(af) the minimum qualification required for admission to a course of degree in law in any recognised University;

(ag) the class or category or persons entitled to be enrolled as advocates;

(ah) the conditions subject to which an advocate shall have the right to practise and the circumstances under which a person shall be deemed to practise as an advocate in a Court;

(b) the form in which an application shall be made for the transfer of the name of an advocate from one State roll to another;

(c) the standards of professional conduct and etiquette to be observed by advocates;

(d) the standards of legal education to be observed by Universities in India and the inspection of Universities for that purpose;

(e) the foreign qualifications in law obtained by persons other than citizens of India which shall be recognised for the purpose of admission as an advocate under this Act;

(f) the procedure to be followed by the disciplinary committee of a State Bar Council and by its own disciplinary committee;

(g) the restrictions in the matter of practise to which senior advocates shall be subject;

(gg) the form of dresses or robes to be worn by advocates, having regard to the climatic conditions, appearing before any Court or tribunal;

(h) the fees which may be levied in respect of any matter under this Act;

(i) general principles for guidance of State Bar Councils and the manner in which directions issued or orders made by the Bar Council of India may be enforced;

(j) any other matter which may be prescribed:

Provided that **no rules** made with reference to clause (c) or clause (gg) shall have effect unless they have been approved by the Chief Justice of India: [Provided further that] no rules made with reference to clause (e) shall have effect unless they have been approved by the Central Government.

(2) Notwithstanding anything contained in the first proviso to sub-section (1) any rules made with reference to clause (c) or clause (gg) of the said sub-section and in force immediately before the commencement of the Advocate (Amendment) Act, 1973 shall continue in force until altered or repealed or amended in accordance with the provisions of this Act.

(a) Section 49 renumbered as sub-section (i) thereof by Act 60 of 1973, S. 38 (31.1.1974).

(b) Substituted for the original clause (a) by Act 21 of 1964, S. 20(a) (16.5.1964).

(c) Substituted for the original clause (af) by Act 60 of 1973, S. 38 (31.1.1974).

(d) Inserted, *ibid.*

(e) Substituted for the original clause (i) by Act 21 of 1964, S. 2(b) (16.5.1964).

(f) Proviso inserted by Act 60 of 1973, S. 38 (31.1.1974).

(g) For words "provided that" words "provided further that" substituted, *ibid.*

(h) Sub-section (2) inserted, *ibid.,* S. 38(3).

49A. Power of Central Government to make rules.—(1) The Central government may, by notification in the Official Gazette, make rules for carrying out the purposes of this Act including rules with respect to any matter for which the Bar Council of India or a State Bar Council has power to make rules.

(2) In particular and without prejudice to the generality of the foregoing power, such rules may provide for—

(a) qualifications for membership of a Bar Council and disqualifications for such membership;

(b) the manner in which the Bar Council of India may exercise supervision and control over State Bar Councils and the manner in which the directions issued or orders made by the Bar Council of India may be enforced;

(c) the class or category of persons entitled to be enrolled as advocates under this Act;

(d) the category of persons who may be exempted from undergoing a course of training and passing an examination prescribed under clause (d) of sub-section (1) of Section 24;

(e) the manner in which seniority among advocates may be determined;

(f) the procedure to be followed by a disciplinary committee of a Bar Council in hearing cases and the procedure to be followed by a disciplinary committee of the Bar Council of India in hearing appeals;

(g) any other matter which may be prescribed.

(3) Rule under this section may be made either for the whole of India or for all or any of the Bar Councils.

(4) If any provision of a rule made by a Bar Council is repugnant to any provision of a rule made by the Central Government under this section, then, the rule under this section, whether made before or after the rule made by the Bar Council shall prevail and the rule made by the Bar Council shall, to the extent of the repugnancy, be void.

(5) Every rule made under this section shall be laid, as soon as may be after it is made, before each House of Parliament, while it is in session, for a total period of thirty days which may be comprised in one session or in two or more successive sessions, and if, before the expiry of the session immediately following the session or the successive sessions aforesaid, both Houses agree in making any modification in the rule or both Houses agree that the rule should not be made, the rule shall thereafter have effect only in such modified form or be of no effect, as the case may be, so however, that any such modification or annulment shall be without prejudice to the validity of, anything previously done under that rule.)

(a) Inserted by Act 21 of 1964, S. 21 (16.5.64).

(b) For such notification see S.O. 926 G.L., 8.3.1968, Pt. II, S. 3(h), Ext., p. 315 as am. by S.O. 1560/ 1969, and S.O. 4101 dt. 30.12.70.

(c) Substituted for original sub-section (5) by Act 60 of 1973, S. 39 (31.1.1974).

50. Repeal of certain enactments.—(a) On the date on which a State Bar Council is constituted under this Act, the provisions of Sections 3 to 7 (inclusive), sub-sections (1), (2) and (3) of S. 9, S. 15, S. 20 of the

Indian Bar Councils Act, 1926, shall stand repealed in the territory for which the State Bar Council is constituted.

(2) On the date on which Chapter III comes into force, the following shall stand repealed, namely:

(a) Sections 6, 7, 18 and 37 of the Legal Practitioners Act, 1879, and so much of Sections 8, 9, 16, 17, 19 and 41 of that Act as relate to the admission and enrolment of legal practitioners;

(b) Sections 3, 4, and 6 of the Bombay Pleaders Act, 1920;

(c) So much of Section 8 of the Indian Bar Councils Act, 1926, as relates to the admission and enrolment of legal practitioners;

(d) the provisions of the Letters Patent of any High Court and of any other law in so far as they relate to the admission and enrolment of legal practitioners.

(3) On the date on which Chapter IV comes into force, the following shall stand repealed, namely:

(a) Sections 4, 5, 10 and 20 of the Legal Practitioners Act, 1879, and so much of Sections 8, 9, 19 and 41 of that Act as confer on legal practitioners that right to practise in any Court or before any authority or person;

(b) Sections 5, 6, 8 and 9 of the Bombay Pleaders Act, 1920;

(c) Section 14 of the Indian Bar Councils Act, 1926, and so much of Sections 8 and 15 of that Act as confer on legal practitioners the right to practise in any Court or before any authority or person;

(d) the Supreme Court Advocates (Practise in High Courts) Act, 1951;

(e) the provisions of the Letters Patent of any High Court and of other law conferring on legal practitioners the right to practise in any Court or before any authority or person.

(4) On the date on which Chapter V comes into force, the following shall stand repealed, namely:

(a) Sections 12 to 15 (inclusive), Sections 21 to 24 (inclusive) and Sections 39 and 40 of the Legal Practitioners Act, 1879, and so much of Sections 16, 17 and 41 of the Act, as relate to the suspension, removal or dismissal of legal practitioners;

(b) Sections 24 to 27 (inclusive) of the Bombay Pleaders Act, 1920;

(c) Sections 10 to 13 (inclusive) of the Indian Bar Councils Act, 1926;

(d) the provisions of the Letters Patent of any High Court and of any other law in so far as they relate to the suspension, removal or dismissal of legal practitioners.

(5) When the whole of this Act has come into force—

(a) the remaining provisions of the Acts referred to in this section which do not stand repealed by virtue of any of the foregoing provisions of this section (except sections 1, 3 and 36 of the Legal Practitioners Act, 1879) shall stand repealed;

(b) the enactments specified in the Schedule shall stand repealed to the extent mentioned therein.

(a) Sub-section (1) of Section 50 was brought into force on 15.12.1961, Gaz. bid., 1961, Extra, Pt. II, Sec. 3(ii), p. 1745.

(b) Dates on which the State Bar Councils were set up are as follows:

The Bar Council of Madras	11th November 1961
The Bar Council of Orissa	11th November, 1961
The Bar Council of Andhra Pradesh	20th November 1961
The Bar Council of Kerala	2nd December, 1961
The Bar Council of Mysore	3rd December, 1961
The Bar Council of Assam	15th December, 1961
The Bar Council of Punjab (Haryana)	16th December, 1961
The Bar Council of Gujarat	16th December, 1961
The Bar Council of Uttar Pradesh	17th December, 1961
The Bar Council of Rajasthan	22nd December, 1961
The Bar Council of Maharashtra	28th December, 1961
The Bar Council of Madhya Pradesh	13th January, 1962
The Bar Council of Bihar	16th January, 1962
The Bar Council of Delhi	22nd January, 1962
The Bar Council of West Bengal	17th April, 1962
The Bar Council of Himachal Pradesh	17th November, 1971

For the areas covered by the Councils, see S. 3.

(c) Sub-section (2) of section 50 was brought into force on 1.12.1961, *ibid.*, p. 1723.

(d) Chap. V was brought into force on 1.9.1963, G.I., 1963, Pt. II, S. 3(ii), Ext., p. 513.

51. Rule of construction.—On and from the appointed day references in any enactment to an advocate enrolled by a High Court in any form of words shall be construed as references to an advocate enrolled under this Act.

(a) Section 51 was brought into force on 24.1.1962—Gaz. Ind., 1962, Extra, Pt. II, Sec. 3(ii), p. 1969.

52. Saving.—Nothing in this act shall be deemed to affect the powers of the Supreme Court to make rules under Article 145 of the Constitution—

(a) for laying down the conditions subject to which a senior advocate shall be entitled to practise in that Court;

(b) for determining the persons who shall be entitled to act in that Court;

(a) Section 52 was brought into force on 24.1.1962, Gaz. Ind., 1962, Extra Pt. II, Sec. 3(h), 169.

CHAPTER VII
TEMPORARY AND TRANSITIONAL PROVISIONS

53. **Elections to First State Bar Council.**—Notwithstanding anything contained in this Act, the elected members of a State Bar Council, constituted for the first time under this Act, shall be elected by and from amongst advocates, Vakils, pleaders and attorneys who, on the date of the election, are entitled as of right to practise in the High Court and are ordinarily practising within the territory for which the Bar Council is to be constituted.

Explanation.—Where the territory for which the Bar Council is to be constituted includes a Union territory, the expression "High Court" shall include the Court of the Judicial Commissioner of that Union territory.

(a) Chapter VII was brought into force on 16.8.1961, Gaz. Ind., 1961, Extra, Pt. II, Sec. 3(h), p. 1237.

54. **Term of office of members of first Bar Council of India and State Bar Councils.**—Notwithstanding anything contained in this Act, the term of office of the elected members of a State Bar Council constituted for the first time, shall be two years from the date of the first meeting of the Council:

[Provided that such members shall continued to hold office until the State Bar Council is reconstituted in accordance with the provisions of this Act].

(a) The words "nominated" and were omitted by the Advocates (Amendment) Act, 1962 (XIV of 1962), S. (30.3.1962).

(b) Words "the Bar Council of India and" were omitted and deemed always to have been so, by Act 21 of 1964, S. 22(1).

(c) Inserted and deemed to have always been inserted by Act 21 of 1964, S. 22(h).

55. **Rights of certain existing legal practitioners not affected. —**

(a) Notwithstanding anything contained in this Act. — Before the dates on which Chapter IV comes into force (hereinafter in this section referred as the said date) by virtue of the provisions of the legal Practioners Act, 1879, the Bombay Pleaders Act, 1920, or any other law who does not elect to be, or is not qualified to be, enrolled as an advocate under this Act;

(b) Omitted.

(c) every mukhtar practising as such immediately before the said date by virtue of the provisions of the Legal Practitioners Act, 1879, or any other law, who does not elect to be, or is not qualified to be, enrolled as an advocate under this act;

(d) every revenue agent practising as such immediately before the said date by virtue of the provisions of the Legal Practitioners Act, 1879, or any other Law; shall, notwithstanding the repeal by this Act of the relevant provisions of the Legal Practitioners Act, 1879, the Bombay Pleaders Act, 1920, or other Law, continue to enjoy the same rights as respect practice in any court or revenue office or before any authority or person and be subject to the disciplinary jurisdiction of the same authority which he enjoyed or, as the case may be, to which he was subject immediately before the said date and accordingly the relevant provisions of the Act or law aforesaid shall have effect in relation to such persons as if they had not been repealed.

(a) Substituted for the original clause (c) by Act 21 of 1964, S. 23 (15.5.1964).

(b) Sub-clause (b) omitted by Act 107 of 1976, S. 10 (15.10.1976).

56. Dissolution of existing Bar Councils.—(1) On the constitution under this Act of a State Bar Council, other than the Bar Council of Delhi (hereinafter referred to as the new Bar Council)—

(a) all properties and assets vesting in the corresponding Bar Council shall vest in the new Bar Council;

(b) all rights, liabilities, and obligations of the corresponding Bar Council, whether arising out of any contract or otherwise, shall be the rights, liabilities and obligations respectively of the new Bar Council;

(c) all proceedings pending before the corresponding Bar Council in respect of all disciplinary matter or otherwise shall stand transferred to the New Bar Council.

(2) In this section, "Corresponding Bar Council" in relation to a State Bar Council, other than the Bar Council of Delhi, means the Bar Council for the High Court in the territory for which the State Bar Council is constituted under this Act.

58. Special provisions during the transitional period.—(1) Where a State Bar Council so constituted is unable to perform its functions by reason of any order or court or otherwise, the functions of that Bar Council or of any committee thereof, in so far as they relate to the admission and enrolment of advocates, shall be performed by the High Court in accordance with the provisions of this Act.

(2) Until Chapter IVB comes into force, a State Bar Council or a High Court performing the functions of a State Bar Council may enrol any person to be an advocate on a state roll, if he is qualified to be so enrolled under this Act, notwithstanding that no rules have been made under Section 28 or that the rules so made have not been approved by the Bar Council of India, and every person so enrolled shall, until that Chapter comes into force, be entitled to all the rights of practice conferred on an advocate under section 14 of the Indian Bar Councils Act, 1926.

(3) Notwithstanding anything contained in this Act, every person who, immediately before the 1st day of December 1961, was an advocate on the roll of any High Court under the Indian Bar Councils Act, 1926 or who has been enrolled as an advocate under this Act shall, until Chapter IV comes into force, be entitled as of right to practise in the Supreme Court, subject to the rules made by the Supreme Court in this behalf.

(3) Notwithstanding the appeal by sub-section (2) of Section 50 of the provisions of the Legal Practitioners Act, 1879 or of the Bombay Pleaders Act, 1920, [or of any other law relating to the admission and enrolment of legal practitioners, the provisions of the Acts, and law aforesaid and any rules made thereunder in so far as they relate to the renewal or the issue by way of renewal) of a certificate to a legal practitioner authorising him to practice shall have effect until Chapter IV comes into force and, accordingly, every certificate issued or renewed to a legal practitioner [who is not enrolled as an advocate under this Act, which is or purports to be issued or renewed under the provisions of either or the aforesaid Acts [or of the other law] during the period beginning with the 1st day of December, 1961 and ending with the date on which Chapter IV comes into force, shall be deemed to have been validly issued or renewed].

(a) Inserted and deemed always to have been inserted by the Advocate (Amendment) Act, 1962 (XIV of 1962), S. 4.

(b) Inserted and deemed always to have been inserted for original words by Act 32 of 1962, S. 3.

(c) Substituted for the words "the issue and renewal" by Act 21 of 1964, S. 25 (16.5.1964).

58A. Special provisions with respect to certain advocates.—(1) Notwithstanding anything contained in this Act, all advocates who, immediately before the 26th day of July, 1948, were entitled to practise in the High Court in Allahabad or the Chief Court in Oudh and who under the provisions of the United Province High Courts (Amalgamation) Order, 1948 were recognised as advocates entitled to practise in the new High Court of Judicature at Allahabad but whose names were not formally entered on the roll of advocates of that High Court merely by reason of the non-payment of the fee payable to the Bar Council of the said High Court and all advocates who were enrolled as such between the said date and the 26th day of May, 1952, shall, for the purposes of Clause (a) of sub-section (1) of Section 17, be deemed to be persons who were entered as advocates on the roll of the said High Court under the Indian Bar Councils Act, 1926 and every such person may, on any application being made in this behalf, be admitted as an advocate on the State roll of Uttar Pradesh.

(2) Notwithstanding anything contained in this Act, all advocates who immediately before the 10th day of October, 1952, were entitled to practise in the High Court of Hyderabad but whose names were not formally entered on the roll of advocates of the High Court merely by reason of the non-payment of the fee payable to the Bar Council of the said High Court shall, for the purposes of clause (a) of sub-section (1) of section 17, be deemed to be persons who were entered as advocates on the roll of the said High Court under the Indian Bar Councils Act, 1926 and every such person may, on an application being made in this behalf, be admitted as an advocate on the State roll of Andhra Pradesh or of Maharashtra.

(3) Notwithstanding anything contained in this Act, all advocates who, immediately before the 1st day of May, 1960, were entitled to practise in the High Court of Bombay and who applied to get their names entered on the roll of advocates of the High Court of Gujarat under the provisions of Section 8 of the Indian Bar Council Act, 1926 but whose names were not so entered by reason of the repeal of the said provision shall, for the purposes of clause (a) of sub-section (1) of Section 17, be deemed to be persons who were entered as advocates on the roll of the High Court of Gujarat under the said Act and every such person may, on an application being made in this behalf, be admitted as an advocate on the State roll maintained in respect of the union territory.

(4) Notwithstanding anything contained in this Act, all persons who, immediately before the 1st day of December, 1961, were advocates

on the roll of the Court of Judicial Commissioner in any Union territory under any law in force in that territory shall, for the purposes of Clause (a) of sub-section (1) of Section 17, be deemed to be persons who were entered as advocates on the roll of a High Court under the Indian Bar Councils Act, 1926 and every such person may, on an application made in this behalf, be admitted as an advocate on the State roll maintained in respect of that Union territory.

(a) Sections 58BA and 58B, inserted by Act 21 of 1964, S. 25 (16.5.1964).

58AA. Special provisions in relation to the Union Territory of Pondicherry.—(1) Notwithstanding anything contained in this Act, all persons who, immediately before the date on which the provisions of the Chapter III are brought into force in the Union territory of Pondicherry, were entitled to practise the profession of law (whether by way of pleading or acting or both) under any law in force in the union territory or who would have been so entitled had they not been in public service on the said date, shall for the purposes of clause (a) of sub-section (1) of Section 17, be deemed to be persons who were entered as advocates on the roll of a High Court under the Indian Bar Councils Act, 1926 and ever such person may, on an application made in this behalf within such time as may be prescribed by the Bar Council of Madras, be admitted as an advocate on the State roll maintained in respect of the said Union territory.

(2) Notwithstanding anything contained in this Act, every oerson who, immediately before the date on which the provisions of Chapter IV are brought into force in the Union territory of Pondicherry, was practising the profession of law (whether by way of pleading or acting or both or in any other way) by virtue of the provisions of any law in force in the said Union territory, who does not elect to be or is not qualified to be enrolled as an advocate under sub-section (1), shall, notwithstanding the repeal of the relevant provisions of such law by the Pondicherry (Extension of Laws) Act, 1968, continue to enjoy the same rights as respects practise in any Court or revenue office or before any authority or person and be subject to the disciplinary jurisdiction of the same authority which he enjoyed, or, as the case may be, to which he was subject, immediately before the said date and accordingly the relevant provisions of the law aforesaid shall have effect in relation to such persons as if they had not been repealed.

(a) Inserted by the Pondicherry (Extension of Laws) Act, 1968 (26 of 1968),

(b) Ch. III and Ch. IV were enforced in the Union Territory of Pondicherry on 10.6.1968—See Pondicherry Gaz., 7.6.1968, Ext. (No. 52).

58AB. Special provisions with respect to certain persons enrolled by Mysore State Bar Council.—Notwithstanding anything contained in this Act or any judgement, decree or order any court or any resolution passed or direction given by the Bar Council of India, every person who was admitted as an advocate on the State roll by the State Bar Council of Mysore during the period beginning with the 28th day of February, 1963, and ending on the 31st day of March, 1964, on the basis of his having obtained a certificate of pleadership from the High Court of Mysore shall, save as otherwise provided, be deemed to have been validly admitted as an advocate on that State roll and accordingly entitled to practise the profession of law (whether by way of pleading or acting or both):

Provided that where any such person has elected to be enrolled as an advocate on the roll of any other State Bar Council, his name shall be deemed to have been struck off the roll of the State Bar Council of Mysore from the date he was enrolled by the State Bar Council:

Provided further that the seniority of such person, whether his name is borne on the State roll of the State Bar Council of Mysore, or on the State roll of any other Bar Council, shall, for the purposes of clause (d) of sub-section (3) of Section 17, be determined by reckoning the 16th day of May, 1964, as the date of admission.

(a) Inserted by Act 33 of 1968, S. 3 (w.e.f. 5.6.1968).

58AC. Special provisions with respect to certain persons enrolled by Uttar Pradesh State Bar Council.—Notwithstanding anything contained in this Act or any judgement decree or order of any court, every person who was enrolled as an advocate by the High Court during the period beginning with the 2nd day of January, 1962 and ending on the 25th day of May, 1962, and was subsequently admitted as an advocate on the State roll by the State Bar Council of Uttar Pradesh shall be deemed to have been validly admitted as an advocate on that State roll from the date of his enrolment by the High Court and accordingly entitled to practise the profession of law (whether by way of pleading or acting or both).

58AD. Special provisions with respect to certain persons migrating to India.—Notwithstanding the repeal by this Act of the provision of the Legal Practitioners Act, 1879, or of any other law relating to the admission and enrolment of legal practitioners (hereafter in this section referred to as such Act or law), every person who migrates to the territory of India from any area which before the 15th day of August, 1947, was comprised within India as defined in the Government of India Act, 1935, and who has, before such migration, been a pleader, mukhtar or revenue agent in any such area under any law in force therein, may be admitted and enrolled under the relevant provisions of such Act or law as a pleader, mukhtar or, as the case may be, revenue agent, if he—

(a) makes an application for the purpose to the appropriate authority under such Act or law; and

(b) is a citizen of India and fulfils other conditions, if any, specified in this behalf by appropriate authority aforesaid, and notwithstanding the repeal by this Act of the relevant provisions of such Act or law, every pleader, mukhtar or revenue agent so enrolled shall have the same rights as respects practice in any court or revenue office or before any other authority or person and be subject to the disciplinary jurisdiction of the same authority to which he would be subject under the relevant provisions of such Act or law as if they had not been repealed and accordingly, those provisions shall have effect in relation to such persons.

58AE. Special provisions in relation to the Union territory of Goa, Daman and Diu.—(1) Notwithstanding anything contained in this Act all persons who, immediately before the date on which the provisions of Chapter HI are brought into force in the Union territory of Goa, Daman and Diu were entitled to practise the profession of law (whether by way of pleading or acting or both) under any law in force in the said Union territory or who would have been so entitled had they not been in public service on the said date, shall, for the purpose of clause (a) of sub-section (1) of Section 17, be deemed to be persons who were entered as advocates on the roll of a High Court under the Indian Bar Councils Act, 1926 and every such person may, on an application made in this behalf within such time as may be specified by the Bar Council of Maharashtra, be admitted as an advocate on the State roll maintained in respect of the said Union territory:

Provided that the provisions of this sub-section shall not apply to any person who, on the date of the application aforesaid, was not a citizen of India.

(2) Notwithstanding anything contained in this Act, every person who, immediately before the date on which the provisions of Chapter IV are brought into force in the Union territory of Goa, Daman and Diu,

was practising the profession of law (whether by way of pleading or acting or both or in any other way) by virtue of the provisions of any law in force in the said Union territory, or who does riot elect to be or is not qualified to be enrolled as an advocate under sub-section (1) shall, notwithstanding the repeal by this Act of the relevant provisions of such law, continue to enjoy the same rights as respects practice in any court or revenue office or before any other authority or person and be subject to the disciplinary jurisdiction of the same authority which he enjoyed or, as the case may be, to which he was subject, immediately before the said date and accordingly the relevant provisions of the law aforesaid shall have effect in relation to such persons as if they had not been repealed.

(3) On the date on which this Act or any part thereof comes into force in the Union territory of Gao, Daman and Diu the law in force in that Union territory which corresponds to this Act or such part and which does not stand repealed by virtue of the provisions of Section 50 of this Act, shall also stand repealed.

58AF. Special provisions in relation to Jammu and Kashmir.— (1) Notwithstanding anything contained in this Act, all advocates who immediately before the date on which the provisions of Chapter III are brought into force into the State of Jammu and Kashmir, were entitled to practise in the High Court of that State, or who would have been so entitled had they not been in public service on the said day, shall, for the purpose of clause (a) of sub-section (1) of Section 17, be deemed to be persons who were entered as advocates on the roll of a High Court under the Indian Bar Councils Act, 1926, and every such person may, on an application made in this behalf within such time as may be specified by the Bar Council of India, be admitted as an advocate on the State roll maintained in respect of the said State.

(2) Notwithstanding anything contained in this Act, every person who, immediately before the date on which the provisions of Chapter III are brought into force in the State of Jammu and Kashmir, was entitled otherwise than as an advocate to practise the profession of law (whether by way of pleading or acting or both) by virtue of the provisions of any law in force in the said State, or who would have been so entitled had he not been in public service on the said date, may be admitted as an advocate on the State roll maintained in respect of the said State, if he—

(i) makes an application for such amendment in accordance with, the provisions of this Act; and

(ii) fulfils the conditions specified in clauses (a), (b), (e) and (f) of sub-section (1) of Section 24.

(3) Notwithstanding anything contained in this Act, every person who immediately before the date on which the provisions of Chapter IV are brought into force in the State of Jammu and Kashmir, was practising the profession of law (whether by way of pleading or acting or both or in any other way) by virtue of the provisions of any law in force therein, or who does not elect to be or is not qualified to be enrolled as an advocate under sub-section (1), or sub-section (2), shall, notwithstanding the repeal by this Act of the relevant provisions of such law, continue to enjoy the same rights as respects practice in any court or revenue office or before any other authority which he enjoyed, or, as the case may be, to which he was subject, immediately before the said date and accordingly the relevant provisions of the law aforesaid shall have effect in relation to such persons as if they had not been repealed.

(4) On the date on which this Act or any part thereof comes into force in the State of Jammu and Kashmir, the law in force in that State which corresponds to this Act or such part thereof which does not stand repealed by virtue of the provisions of Section 50 of this Act, shall also stand repealed.

(a) Sections 58AC, 58AD, 58AF inserted by Act 60 of 1973, S. 40 (31-1-1974).

58AG. Special provisions in relation to articled clerks.—Notwithstanding anything contained in this Act, every person who, immediately before the 31st day of December, 1976, has commenced his articleship and passed the preliminary examination, for the purpose of enrolment as an attorney of the High Court at Calcutta in accordance with the rules made under sub-section (2) of Section 34, before the omission of that sub-section by the Advocates (Amendment) Act, 1976, may be admitted as an advocate on the State roll if he:

(i) passes, on or before the 31st day of December, 1980:

(a) the Final examination in a case where such person has, before the 31st day of December, 1976, passed the Intermediate examination.

(b) the Intermediate and the Final examinations in any other case.

Explanation.—For the purpose of this clause, the High Court at Calcutta may prescribe such rules as may be necessary under sub-section (2) of Section 34, specifying the nature of the examinations and any other matter relating thereto,

(ii) makes an application for such enrolment in accordance with the provisions of this Act; and

(iii) fulfils the conditions specified in clauses (a), (b), (e) and (f) for sub-section (1) or Section 24.

(a) Section 58AG inserted by Act 38 of 1977, S. 7 (31-10-1977).

58B. Special provision relating to certain disciplinary proceedings.—(1) As from the 1st day of September, 1963, every proceeding in respect of any disciplinary matter in relation to any existing advocate of a High Court shall, save as provided in the first proviso to sub-section (2), be disposed of by the State Bar Council in relation to that High Court, as if the existing advocate had been enrolled as an advocate on its roll.

(2) If immediately before the said date, there is any proceeding in respect of any disciplinary matter in relation to an existing advocate pending before any High Court under the Indian Bar Councils Act, 1926, such proceeding shall stand transferred to the State Bar Councils Act, 1926, such proceeding shall stand transferred to the State Bar Council in relation to that High "Court, as if it were a proceeding pending before the corresponding Bar Council under clause (c) of sub-section (1) of Section 56:

Provided that where in respect of any such proceeding the High Court has received the finding of a Tribunal constituted under Section 11 of the Indian Bar Councils Act, 1926, the High Court shall dispose of the case and it shall be lawful for the High Court to exercise for the purpose all powers conferred on it under Section 12 of the said Act as if that section had not been repealed:

Provided further that where the High Court has referred back any case for further inquiry under sub-section (4) of Section 12 of the said Act, the proceeding shall stand transferred to the State Bar Council in relation to the High Court as if it were a proceeding pending before the corresponding Bar Council under Clause (c) of sub-section (1) of Section 56.

(3) If immediately before the said date there is any proceeding in respect of any disciplinary matter depending in relation to any pleader, vakil, mukhtar or attorney, who has been enrolled as an advocate on any State roll under the Act, such proceeding shall stand transferred to the State Bar Council on the roll of which he has been enrolled and be dealt with under this Act as if it were a proceeding arising against him thereunder.

(4) In this section, "existing advocate" means a person who was enrolled as an advocate on the roll of any High Court under the Indian Bar Council disciplinary matter is initiated against him, is not enrolled as an advocate on a State roll under this Act.

(5) The provisions of this section shall have effect, notwithstanding anything contained in this Act.

(a) Sections 58A and 58B, inserted by Act 21 of 1964, S. 25 (16-5-1964).

59. Removal of difficulties.—(1) If any difficulty arises in giving effect to the provisions of this Act, particularly in relation to the transition from the enactments repealed by this Act, the Central Government may, by order published in the Official Gazette, make such provisions not inconsistent with the purposes of this Act, as appear to it to be necessary or expedient for removing the difficulty.

(2) An order under sub-section (1) may be made so as to have retrospective effect from a date not earlier than the 1st day of December, 1961.

(a) Inserted and deemed always to have been so inserted, by the Advocates (Amendment Act, 1962 (XIV of 1962)), S.4.

(b) The following are such orders passed so far:—

(1) Advocates (Removal of Difficulties) Order No. 2,1963 (1.9.1963), G.I., 31.8.63, Pt. II, S. 3(ii), Ext., p. 513.

(2) Advocates (Removal of Difficulties) Order No. 2, 1963, (1.10.1963), G.I., 21.12.1963, Pt. II, S. 3(ii), Ext, p. 879.

(3) Advocates (Removal of Difficulties) Order, 1966 (w.e.f. 1.11.1965), G-I., 10.1.1966, Pt. II, S. 3(ii), Ext, p. 7.

(4) Advocates (Removal of Difficulties) Order, 1968 (Enforcement at once, G.I., 23.2.1968, Pt. II, S. 3(ii), Ext., p. 127.

60. Power of Central Government to make rules.—(1) Until rules in respect of matter under this Act are made by a State Bar Council and approved by the Bar Council of India, the power to make rules in respect of that matter shall be exercisable by the Central Government.

(2) The Central Government after consultation with the Bar Council of India may, by notification in the Official Gazette, make rules under sub-section (1) either for any State Bar Council or generally for all State Bar Councils and the rules so made shall have effect, notwithstanding anything contained in this Act;

(3) Where in respect of any mater any rules are made by the Central Government under this section for any State Bar Council, and in respect

of the same matter, rules are made by the State Bar Council and approved by the Bar Council of India, the Central Government may, by notification in the Official Gazette, direct that the rules made by it in respect of such matter shall cease to be in force in relation to that Bar Council with effect from such date as may be specified in the notification and on the issue of such notification, the rules made by the Central Government shall, accordingly, cease to be in force except as respects things done or omitted to be done before the said date.

(a) Inserted by Act 32 of 1962, S. 4 (14.9.1964).

Annexure - II

REPORT OF THE WORKING GROUP ON LEGAL EDUCATION

BACKGROUND

1. The National Knowledge Commission ("NKC") was established by the Prime Minister of India in 2005 to recommend and undertake reforms in order to make India a knowledge-based economy and society. An important constituent of the NKC's functions is professional education, particularly in the field of legal education. In light of its significance, the NKC constituted a Working Group on legal education in the country. The members nominated by the Chairperson of the NKC, Mr. Sam Pitroda, to the Working Group are Justice Jagannadha Rao (Chair), Justice Leila Seth, Dr. Madhav Menon, Dr. B.S. Chimni, Dr. Mohan Gopal, Mr. P.P. Rao and Mr. Nishith Desai.

2. The Terms of Reference of the Working Group are as follows:

   (a) Identify constraints, problems and challenges relating to curriculum, teaching, infrastructure, administration and access.

   (b) Recommend changes and reforms to address the problems and challenges relating to curriculum, teaching, infrastructure, administration, and access.

   (c) Explore methods of attracting and retaining talented faculty members.

   (d) Suggest measures to develop a research tradition in faculties of law and law schools.

   (e) Suggest innovative means of raising standards and promoting excellence in legal education situated in the wider social context.

(f) Suggest ways of incorporating emerging fields of legal education in teaching and curricula.

(g) Identify problems implicit in regulatory structures that constrain the quality and spread of legal education.

(h) Examine any other issue that may be relevant in this context.

3. The Working Group met on the following dates: September 24, 2006, October 5, 2006, November 12, 2006, January 15, 2007 and January 30, 2007.

4. The members of the Working Group circulated several notes for discussion and minutes of the meetings were prepared at the end of each meeting and circulated. The various aspects covered by the Terms of Reference were discussed in detail and it was found that some of these aspects overlap each other. Therefore, the Working Group has identified the following topics of importance in the matter of legal education:

I. Vision and goals of legal education — status today, road map and broad strategy to reach those goals

(a) At least one centre of legal excellence in every state.

(b) Broad-based content and scope of legal education in the context of constitutional goals.

(c) Restructuring governance of legal education system accordingly.

(d) Regional and Advanced Centres of legal research excellence to advance policy development/teacher training/generating new knowledge.

II. Content and scope of legal education (Multisdisciplinary and based in social context)

(a) Curriculum planning and development.

(b) Teaching materials.

(c) Teaching/learning methods.

(d) Skills education/training with emphasis on experiential learning.

(e) Ethics/values for multiple roles.

(f) Examination.

(g) Legal knowledge management through legal education grid through Information and Communication Technologies ("ICT") and distance learning.

III. Governance Structure

(a) Strict and professional control for quality.

(b) Selection and service conditions.

(c) Academic freedom.

(d) Admission norms-procedures/access-needs blind; need fulfilled admissions.

(e) Financing legal education — state financing for meritorious students/ deserving colleges in rural areas.

(f) Accreditation, monitoring, accountability.

IV. At least four independent research centers to be funded by the central government with investment of ₹ 100 crore each and the following objectives:

(a) Social justice promotion/judicial policy.

(b) Processual justice for better justice delivery.

(c) Dissemination of new knowledge/journals.

(d) Research methodology including empirical methods.

(e) Integration of research-based learning.

(f) Judicial/court/legal aid administration/management.

(g) Alternative Dispute Resolution ("ADR")/conflict resolution.

(h) International law/comparative/globalization.

(i) Shaping systemic legal change including indigenous traditions.

(j) Teacher training-library development/continuity education.

V. Access, finance, infrastructure and management

(a) Support to students admitted on merit (loans and scholarships).

(b) Ensuring every law school admitting 100 students annually has the resources to meet an annual expenditure of ₹ 5 crore.

(c) Representation of bar, bench, academia and students in management.

CHAPTER I
VISION AND GOALS

1.1 Some key statistics on legal education are pertinent towards the understanding the state of legal education in India today.

(a) Total number of students admitted for legal education every year for 2000-01: 63,381 (latest figures not available)

(b) Total number of law graduates admitted to the bar every year in

- 2002 : 28,268
- 2003 : 33,657
- 2004 : 46,438

(Figures for 2005 and 2006 not available)

(c) Total number of institutions (all inclusive) teaching law as on October 31, 2006 : 750

(d) Total number of Government institutions: 153

(e) Total number of Private institutions: 586

(f) Total number of National Law School Universities ("NLSU") as on October 31, 2006: 11

(g) Total number of students admitted to the NLSUs in 2006: 936

1.2 The main challenge facing India's legal and judicial system is ensuring that common people in India are able to enjoy their constitutional and legislative rights to the fullest extent. The legal system should also effectively facilitate eradication of poverty as well as equitable and environmentally sustainable economic growth.

1.2.1 To this end, legal education should aim to prepare legal professionals who will play a decisive leadership role in meeting these challenges, not only as advocates practising in courts, but also as legislators, judges, policy makers, public officials and civil society activists as well as legal counsel in the private sector. Legal education should also prepare lawyers to meet the new challenges of working in a globalized knowledge economy in which the nature and organization of law and legal practice are undergoing a paradigm shift. Original and path breaking legal research is needed to create new legal knowledge and legal ideas that will help us to meet these challenges in a manner responsive to the needs of the country and the ideals and goals of our Constitution.

1.2.2 The Working Group is of the opinion that the vision of legal education is to ensure justice-oriented legal education to contribute to the realization of values enshrined in the Constitution of India. Legal education must also inculcate the need to observe the highest standards of professional ethics and a spirit of public service. In order to achieve these goals, legal education needs to be broad-based, multidisciplinary, multifunctional and contextual. The phenomenon of globalization provides an important context in relation to which the vision and goals of legal education have to be concretized.

1.2.3 An important aim of legal education is also to meet the growing demands of the legal services market without undermining the public service character of the law school/university. Legal education must cater to a wider audience than only provide personnel for the purposes of the administration of justice in courts. The new developmental agenda needs knowledge of international practices and transcends the established view that the purpose of legal education is only to generate practising lawyers.

The aim of legal education also should be to create lawyers who are comfortable and skilled in 'dealing' with the differing legal systems and cultures that make up our global community while remaining strong in one's own national legal system.

1.3 A number of law schools have been offering quality legal education. However, the most immediate challenge is to improve the quality of legal education in a vast majority of law schools in the country. This task entails a range of measures including reforms in the existing regulatory structure, significant focus on curriculum development keeping in mind contemporary demands for legal services, recruitment of competent and committed faculty, establishing research and training centers, necessary financial support from the State, and creating necessary infrastructure, especially a well-endowed library.

CHAPTER II

CONTENT AND SCOPE OF LEGAL EDUCATION IN A MULTIDISCIPLINARY CONTEXT

2.1 Admissions

2.1.1 In order to improve the quality of legal education, certain minimum conditions for admission to law schools and universities need to be agreed upon. Some NLSUs have agreed to conduct a common entrance test (CET). Consideration may be given to including other law schools and universities in the CET network. A single common entrance test for both three-year and five-year LL.B. programmes may be devised. For the purposes of admission, including appearing in CET, a minimum percentage of forty-five marks in the class 12/graduation examination may be considered. Law schools may, however, be permitted to set a higher minimum percentage. Once the CET model extends to a large number of law schools, consideration may be given to prescribing a requirement that a candidate secure a minimum percentage of forty-five in the CET for admission.

2.2. Curriculum Development

2.2.1 In order to realize the stated vision and goals of legal education, the curricula and syllabi need to be based in a wider body of social science knowledge. An understanding of the newer areas of law also requires some familiarity with developments in science and technology in addition to other rapidly developing sectors.

2.2.2 Curriculum development *inter alia* involves revisiting the distinction between core/compulsory and optional courses, considering the need to expand the domain of optional courses, rethinking the syllabus of individual courses, and developing innovative pedagogic methods.

2.2.3 At present, the Bar Council of India (BCI) prescribes a certain number of core courses, essentially leaving it to the law school to identify the optional courses to be offered (although the BCI mentions a few). In many NLSUs, up to 40 to 50 optional courses are offered. This development may be usefully extended to the other law schools. For the present, each law school may be required to offer a minimum of twenty-five optional courses. However, autonomy may be given to NLSUs and to the universities, which teach law in the university colleges and to which the private law colleges are affiliated, to decide the core and optional courses to be offered. It is suggested that the percentage of concentration should be as follows: 50% core courses (including legal research and clinic courses) and 50% optional courses.

2.2.4 The syllabi of law courses have to be carefully designed. They must respect the multidisciplinary character of legal education. In this regard, there is a need to keep in view the developments in social and natural sciences. In order to sensitize the law student to the values enshrined in the Constitution of India, it is important to mainstream human rights law. With the advent of globalization, it has become increasingly important to include international and comparative law perspectives.

2.2.5 Modules on issues such as globalization, environmental concerns, new technology, shifting government policies, trade trends, corporate movements, new and prevailing foreign investment avenues and changing labor and employment policies, to mention a few, should be included in the curriculum so that the graduating generation of lawyers can swiftly relate to the real world for the optimum application of legal services. This interweaving of law with the related issues of the contemporary world will add immense value to the law degree.

2.2.6 Legal education must equip the student with the necessary theoretical and practical skills to deal with the diverse and expanding world of legal practice. For example, the law graduate must be able to deal with and respond to a range of complex legal issues and problems, even as he or she chooses to specialize in a particular area of law; he must possess basic "legal" skills including negotiation, advocacy, drafting, counseling and research skills; the law graduate must be in a position to identify, analyze, and synthesize a vast array of legal materials and present it in a concise and logical manner; he must be sufficiently acquainted with the procedural aspects of the legal system so as to be in a position to give practical advice to clients; he must be trained to respond to new/novel problems that call for practical solutions; he must be able to contribute creatively to the range of social problems and challenges that face the nation; he must be trained to research independently so that he/she can contribute to the total pool of legal ideas through research publications; he must be able to read and analyze judicial decisions that are typically long, verbose, complex and difficult to understand, and should possess an ability to skim through passages, understand the relationship between the parts of the passage and also read between the lines — all of which are integral to a lawyer's tasks; he must also be grounded in ethical issues governing the legal profession. In order to imbibe the theoretical and practical skills, the syllabus of individual courses may be framed in consultation with practitioners, including members of the bar, the judiciary, industry and civil society.

2.2.7 To impart these skills, a combination of various teaching methods including lectures, the case-study method, and problem-oriented exercises are required. Imaginative pedagogic methods including field surveys and visits, simulated legal environments, and legal aid clinics may be used. Consideration may be given to evolving a transnational curriculum to be taught jointly by a global faculty through video-conferencing and internet modes.

2.3 Reading Material

2.3.1 An important aspect of curriculum development is the identification of appropriate reading materials, both essential and advanced. Study materials must include a range of readings including social science, science and technology, comparative and international, and human rights material.

2.3.2 The objectives of mainstreaming social sciences literature, human rights law, business law and international and comparative law is to be met. It is recommended that a committee or committees be formed at the law school level that include practitioners, social science faculty, and teachers of human rights law to discuss the syllabus and reading materials of all core and optional courses. It would be helpful in this regard to seek student feedback to understand the deficiencies in the structure and readings of courses offered at present. Thought may be given to setting up an all-India Working Group to devise a "model" syllabus for all core and optional courses. The law schools would be free to use and depart from the "model" syllabus.

2.3.3 So far as professional ethics is concerned, the study material for the course must consist not only of readings that familiarize the student with the basics of professional ethics but also a number of relevant orders passed by the BCI, the State Bar Councils and judgements of the High Courts and the Supreme

Court, in which punishments have been awarded for professional misconduct.

2.4 Clinics

2.4.1 There is an urgent need to revisit and redesign the Clinic Courses. At present, these courses often tend to be soft courses in which a bit of relationship between theory and practice is dealt with (e.g., through some exposure to forensic sciences). There is a need to modernize clinic courses through introducing new areas of law: for example, specialized areas of contract law, Intellectual Property Rights ("IPR") laws, corporate law, etc. may be the subject of clinic courses. There is a need to recruit specialized faculty for the purpose.

2.5 Examination System

2.5.1 The task of curriculum development also includes the designing of appropriate framework for evaluating students. The simple end of the year examination or end semester examination does not encourage necessary analytical, writing and communication skills. Many NLSUs have introduced the idea of project papers, project and subject viva, along with an end semester examination. The different components help develop the ability to carry out independent research and the ability to write and critically evaluate appropriate legal materials. The end semester examination should be problem-oriented and not a system that tests memory.

2.5.2 The credit system of evaluation may be introduced to replace the marks system. Various heads could be given a certain credit value, both course-wise and activity-wise (e.g., participation in Moot Courts, representing the institution in competitive activity related to legal education, joining Legal Aid camps, internships with law firms, research projects, etc).

2.6 Internship

2.6.1 The internship programme is a critical element of professional legal education as it allows practical learning in real world settings from peers. The internship programme that presently exists in many NLSUs, needs to be extended to all other law schools, i.e., where it does not presently exist. In many NLSUs, students have to intern every summer. Over the period of five years, a student in a particular NLSU interns with NGOs, trial courts, appellate courts, law firms and corporate firms. While it may not be easy for students of all law schools to get placement in the chambers of Senior Counsel in the trial and appellate courts, or in law firms and corporate houses, or in NGOs, some amount of internship is absolutely necessary to prepare a graduate for the world of law practice. The BCI and the State Bar Councils could play a catalytic role in facilitating the internship programmes. The internship programme, where it exists can be strengthened through rethinking the period of internship and the need for some amount of structuring through discussions with the bar, judiciary, law firms, corporate houses and NGOs. There is, in other words, some need for standardization of the internship programme to ensure that it does not become a mere ritual.

2.7 Mooting

2.7.1 Mooting is an integral part of legal education. It helps a student hone his/her research and communication skills. It also allows a student to learn legal etiquette so necessary to all forms of legal practice. Therefore, periodic workshops should be held to acquaint the law student with different aspects of mooting. There should also be established formal procedures for selecting teams that represent the law schools in national and international moots.

2.8 Legal Aid

2.8.1 Participation in legal aid programmes should also be an integral part of legal education. It provides a crucial link between the esoteric world of law and the existential world of the ordinary citizen. The idea of holistic legal education would be somewhat incomplete unless a law student is acquainted with the problems of ordinary people.

2.9 Legal Knowledge Dissemination and Management

2.9.1 For the maximum dissemination of legal knowledge across the country, the following may be considered: use of video conferencing of lectures of faculty (within India and outside), availability of computers to a large number of students, access to the internet, networking the information available in the Indian Law Institute ("1LI"), Supreme Court Library, Indian Society for International Law ("1SIL") as well as those of universities and public institutions; availability of free and subscription based data bases. Translation of major legal texts may also be considered for wider dissemination.

2.10 LL.M.

2.10.1 There has been a steady decline in the quality of LL.M. programmes. In the NLSUs, the LL.M. programme is generally neglected although some have started to pay attention to it. There is a need not only to design appropriate courses, study materials, internship programme, systems of evaluation but also to encourage the development of skills necessary for classroom teaching for those wishing to join the academia. In the latter respect, Law Teaching courses may be introduced in the LL.M. programme so that those proposing to do LL.M. are able to assess their inclination/ability for teaching in advance. The writing of a dissertation needs to be made mandatory as a part of the requirements of the LL.M. programme to develop and consolidate research, analytic and writing skills.

2.11 M.Phil. and Ph.D.

2.11.1 Postgraduates in law and the faculty members in law schools must be encouraged to undertake M.Phil. and Ph.D. research. Appropriate incentive schemes, on the lines of the current University Grants Commission ("UGC") scheme, may also be considered. There is need to improve the quality of the M.Phil. and Ph.D. courses. Towards this end, a course in research methodology may be made mandatory for all M.Phil. and Ph.D. students. A pre-registration presentation also has to be introduced as a compulsory measure.

2.12 Measures to develop a research tradition in the legal field

India, in keeping with its status as an emerging economic power, must turn from being a simple consumer of knowledge to a producer of knowledge in order to identify and protect its national interests. India, in other words, needs to be proactive in advancing ideas and proposals in the world of law. For this to happen, law schools and universities need to provide leadership in the field of ideas. It entails much emphasis on research and publications through developing the analytic, research and writing skills of law students. It also calls for encouraging faculty members to undertake research as an integral part of good teaching.

2.12.1 The following measures are *inter alia* necessary for the development of a research tradition in the field of law:

- Emphasizing analytic and writing skills in the LL.B. programme.

- Teaching research methodology as an integral part of the LL.B. programme: learning to formulate a research problem/ question, assemble a bibliography, write a synopsis, and use footnotes.
- Creating excellent and research-friendly library facilities to give students/faculty members easy access to latest materials and developments.
- Providing the faculty with access to computers and internet facilities, the latter being essential to overcome to some extent the lack of a good library.
- Rationalizing the teaching load so as to leave faculty members sufficient time for research.
- Granting sabbatical leave to faculty members to undertake intensive research. M.Phil. and Ph.D. degrees should be rewarded if these result in peer-reviewed publications, either through additional increments (beyond the UGC scheme) or in any other appropriate manner.
- Institutionalizing faculty seminars as these create an environment in which ideas are given importance and the rigor of research tested.
- Organizing periodic conferences on different law subjects with the idea of bringing out publications. Abstracts for such conferences should be invited and carefully chosen so as to ensure the quality of the end product.
- Establishing quality peer-reviewed journals to act as an example for the desirable quality of publications.
- Prescribing research output as one of the criteria for the promotion of faculty members.
- Creating a database of citations so as to identify the most cited and influential writings and considering such data for promotion purposes.
- Setting up advanced centres for legal research. Four such regional centres may be established with a mandate for promoting research. (This issue has been dealt with separately in this report.)

CHAPTER III
GOVERNANCE STRUCTURE

3. Standing Committee on Legal Education

3.1 The Report of the National Knowledge Commission envisages the constitution of a single regulator assisted by several standing committees, including a Standing Committee on Legal Education. Various aspects relating to the present status of Legal Education, the existing regulator, namely, the Bar Council of India (BCI), and constitution of a Standing Committee on Legal education are dealt with in this chapter.

3.2 Changes in legal education in the last fifty years show that the provisions of the Advocates Act, 1961 are no longer sufficient:

3.2.1 Under the Advocates Act, 1961 ("Act"), the role allocated to the BCI was very limited in the sense that it was to promote legal education and to lay down minimum standards with a minimum standard necessary for those students who ultimately enter the legal profession to practice in the courts. The provisions of the Act did not envisage a larger role for the BCI.

3.2.2 The concept before and in 1961 was that law schools should mainly produce graduates for the purpose of entry into the bar. The Advocates Act, 1961 was, therefore, enacted with that objective in mind by Parliament. According to the Supreme Court of India, in **O.N. Mohindroo vs. B.C.I.** (A.I.R. 1968 SC 888 = (1968)3 SCR 709) and **Bar Council of U.P.'s case** (AIR 1973 SC 231 = (1973) I SCC 261 = (1973) 2 SCR 1073) the subject covered by the Advocates Act, 1961 is referable to Entries 77, 78 in List I of Schedule VII of the Constitution of India. These two entries deal, among others, with the subject: "persons entitled to practice before the Supreme Court" (Entry 77) and "persons entitled to practice before the High Court" (Entry 78)".

3.2.3 Under section 7(1)(h) of the Advocates Act, the BCI has been entrusted, as stated above, with the limited role of "promoting legal education and laying down minimum standards of legal education" required for students who "are entitled to practice". Section 7(1)(h) requires the BCI to "consult the universities for the purpose of laying down these standards of legal education". Section 7(1)(i) of the Act enables the BCI to grant recognition to universities whose law degrees shall be sufficient qualification for enrolment as an advocate. The BCI may, for this purpose, visit and inspect the universities concerned whose degrees in law may be recognized for the purpose of enrolment of law graduates as lawyers. Similar power is conferred by Section 6(1)(gg) of the Act on the State Bar Councils in regard to inspection. Section A of Part IV of the Rules made by the BCI deals with the five years' course. Section B deals with the three years' course and Section C deals with inspection.

3.3 Changed Scenario

3.3.1 About fifty years ago, the concept was that the law schools are meant to produce graduates who would mostly come to the bar, while a few may go into law teaching. The Advocates Act, 1961 was enacted to achieve the said object, namely, to prescribe minimum standards for entry into professional practice 'in the courts', as stated above. But during this period and more particularly after liberalization in the year 1991, the entire concept of legal education has changed. Today, legal education has to meet not only the requirements of the bar and the new needs of trade, commerce and industry but also the requirements of globalization. New subjects with international dimensions have come into legal education. There is also an enormous need for non practising law graduates in trade and commerce. It is also necessary to allow engineers, chartered accountants, scientists and doctors to qualify in law for non-practising purposes. Indeed, it is gratifying that some Indian Institute of Technology ("IIT") institutions have recently started several courses in law. The Open University system must also be allowed to cater to legal education. The Bar Council of India may, of course, still deal with the minimum standards of legal education for the purposes of entry into the bar but there is a need to have a new regulatory mechanism which will cater to the above-mentioned present and future needs of the country.

3.3.2 Therefore, among the various types of legal education, we can identify the type which is necessary for those who practice law, the type which prepares them to become researchers and teachers, the type which deals exclusively with academic subjects of substantive law, the type which deals with public legal education or para-legal education, the type that prepares law graduates to deal with legal, regulatory and ethical issues in active sectors of domestic and international business and industry, and finally, the type which professionals in engineering, medicine, management and social work may require. It will be noticed that the Bar Council's role is confined to the first category only.

3.4 Bar Council of India has been conferred limited powers but is exercising more powers under subordinate legislation:

3.4.1 In the light of the concept behind the Advocates Act, 1961, as stated above, very limited powers were conferred on the BCI. But, during the last few decades, inasmuch as there was no other regulator to take care of emerging needs and trends, the BCI has been dealing with all aspects of legal education under Resolutions, Rules and Regulations instead of limiting itself to the maintenance of minimum standards of legal education for the purpose of entry into the bar.

3.4.2 In the 'First National Consultation Conference of Heads of Legal Education Institutions' held on 12.8.2002, it was pointed out as follows: "The regulatory structure for legal education in India is currently seriously flawed and needs careful reconsideration. A typical law college has four masters at a minimum; the university to which it is affiliated; the State Government; the University Grants Commission; and the Bar Council of India...... These four agencies have varying mandates, interests and constituencies and do not provide coherent guidance for the improvement of legal education in the country". It also stated: "There is wide concern among legal academics that they are not adequately consulted currently by any of these authorities". It was also clearly observed in the conference that the BCI had spread its jurisdiction beyond what was contemplated by Entries 77 and 78 of List I of Schedule VII of the Constitution and the provisions of the Advocates Act, 1961. The conference wanted that the BCI concern itself only with the minimum standards necessary for entry into the bar. It said: "The Bar Council of India would then be responsible only for regulating entry into the legal profession and maintenance of professional standards rather than for legal education".

3.4.3 In the last three decades, as stated above, the BCI, by virtue of its Resolutions, Rules and Regulations, has taken over the entire body of powers in relation to legal education which is not the intention of the Advocates Act, 1961, which is a legislation under Entries 77 and 78 of List 1 Schedule VII of the Constitution of India. The BCI, under its powers to grant recognition to universities for the purpose of enrolment of law graduates has been also dealing with inspections, affiliation or disaffiliation of various law colleges, granting annual affiliation or permanent affiliation, etc. It has also been laying down conditions for establishment of law schools, buildings, appointment of faculty, and a variety of other matters in which the faculty and other players have not been allowed to have any effective role. These powers were extended by the BCI under Resolutions, Rules and Regulations, as stated above, though such extension is not permitted by the Advocates Act, 1961.

3.4.4 While the statement of objects and reasons and the preamble of the University Grants Commission Act, 1956 and of the Indian Medical Council Act, 1956 refer to the constitution of bodies for maintaining 'standards of education', there are no such words in the Statement of Objects and Reasons and the Preamble of the Advocates Act, 1961. The Act deals with minimum standards of legal education only in the context of 'practice in courts'. The Supreme Court of India has, in fact, held that the UGC and the Medical Council of India ("MCI"), whose powers deal respectively, with all aspects of education or medical education, can lay down standards of education which will override any other law. See **State of MP vs. Nivedita Jain** AIR 1981 SC 2045 = 1982(1) SCR 759 = (1981)4 SCC 296; **Premchand Jain vs. R.K.Chhabra** AIR 1984 SC 981 - (1984) 2 SCR 883 = (1984) 2 SCC 302, **Osmania University Teachers Association vs. State of AP,** AIR 1987 SC 2034 = (1987) 3 SCR 949 = (1987) 4 SCC 671, **University of Delhi vs. Raj Singh** 1994 Suppl. (3) SCC 516 = AIR (1995) SC 336, **Medical Council of India vs. State of Karnataka** 1998 (6) SCC 131 = AIR 1998 SC 2423; **Dr. Preethi Srivastava and Another vs. State of M.P. and Others** (1999) 7 SCC 120 — AIR 1999 SC 2894. But such a general power to lay down standards of legal education for all purposes has not been conferred on the Bar Council of India by the Advocates Act, 1961.

3.4.5 As pointed out by Prof. Manik Sinha, Dean, Dr. RML Avadh University, in a well-written article titled 'Interference of Bar Council of India in Legal Education: Its Legality and Justifiability' (published in the volume, 'Legal Education in India in the 21st Century', edited by Profs. A.K. Kaul and V.K. Ahuja, p. 241), there appears to be considerable justification for treating the rules/resolutions/circulars of the Bar Council of India dated 2-7-96,21-10-97, 23-9-98,22-12-98 etc., made under way of delegated legislation, taking over maintenance of standards, curriculum, qualifications for admission and for faculty and inspections for all purposes, as being outside the scope of powers and jurisdiction of the Bar Council of India.

3.4.6 The members of the BCI who are practising lawyers and who get elected to the Bar Council, do not all have expert knowledge or experience for deciding the requirements of legal education for purposes other than practice in the courts. Indeed, the Bar Council is not supposed to deal with all aspects of legal education. As pointed in **Sobhana Kumar vs. Mangalore University** (AIR 1985 Karnataka 223) by Rama Jois J (as he then was), the BCI can only prescribe minimum standards for entry into bar whereas the universities or the law colleges can prescribe higher standards. (See also the 141st Report of the Law Commission, 1958 recommendation 25 is at page 550) and the 184th Report of the Law Commission, 2002, para 4.11). As the Advocates Act, 1961 is not intended to cover all aspects of legal education other than entry into the bar, the Rules, Circulars and Resolutions of the Bar Council of India in relation to all other aspects of legal education must be treated as beyond the scope of permissible delegated legislation and therefore invalid.

3.5 There has not been effective consultation between the Bar Council of India and the Faculty:

3.5.1 Further, presently, there is no effective consultation with the faculty. In the Legal Education Committee of the BCI constituted under Section 10(2)(b) of the Act, there are 10 members out of whom five are lawyers — Bar Councilors, a retired Judge of the Supreme Court, a High Court Judge, the Law Secretary and the Secretary, University Grant Commission and there is only one faculty member. Of course, the Law Commission has recommended in the 184th Report (2002) that in the place of the two Secretaries, there could be two more members from the faculty. But, even that is not sufficient. There are more than 700 law schools in the county and it is a grave travesty of justice that the faculty has no equal role in the matter of legal education, whether it deals with entry into the Bar or with the general needs of society for legal services.

3.6 Permissions have been granted to several law schools of poor quality:

3.6.1 The Report of the Ahmadi Committee (1994), constituted by the Chief Justice of India and the various resolutions in other conferences have repeatedly pointed out that the BCI has granted permission to a large number of law schools which are maintaining very poor standards and have very poor infrastructure and several of these colleges are located in remote places, some times not even in the district headquarters. The faculty and library facilities in several of these law colleges are very much deficient. The inspections by the Bar Council's teams appear to have failed in their work. Only a few days ago, the Chief Justice of India observed in Patna that a small place like Junagadh in Gujarat has over thirty law colleges! There are several such situations across the country.

3.7 Most of the seven hundred odd law schools do not compare well with the standards and curriculum required in the present age:

3.7.1 While the NLSUs and some other law schools teach a very large number of subjects both compulsory and optional, which are necessary and useful for a variety of purposes in legal education, the other law schools offer only the minimum number of compulsory subjects prescribed by the Bar Council of India. These other law schools are not able to offer more compulsory or optional subjects because of limited faculty. The NLSUs and few other law schools are offering a larger number of optional subjects, which in some institutions are more than 40. The faculty in these 700 odd law schools is limited because they are either large in number in one place or are located in remote areas in the mofussil where sometimes there is not even a District Court.

3.7.2 Today, we have about 11 NLSUs where students are selected in an all-India competition. These colleges have been producing our best legal talent comparable to the most renowned colleges in U.S and U.K. However, this alone is not sufficient for our purposes and we have to raise the standards of the remaining 700 odd law schools. The Law Commission has indeed observed in its 184th Report (2002) (see para 10.7) as follows:

"We cannot, however, rest content with a few star colleges. We must be concerned with all the rest of the hundreds of law colleges located in cities and district headquarters all over the country. It is these students who come to the bar in great numbers at the grass-root level. A few bright star colleges with limited number of student intake in an All-India selection is not the end and may not result in an overall change in the level of legal education".

3.7.3 Therefore, there is need to bring about a revolutionary change in the standards and curriculum of these 700 and odd law schools so as to bring them, step by step, to the level required in the present age. In fact, it is necessary that all these law schools must be compelled to provide a large number of optional subjects.

3.7.4 A rating system based on a set of agreed criteria (e.g., facilities, course offered, qualifications and experience of instructors, infrastructure, student selection system, salaries paid to teaching staff, etc.) could be developed to gauge the standard of the law schools, and recognition could be either granted or withdrawn on the basis of such ratings. The rating result should be published both in hard copy and online, and should be reviewed on an annual basis.

3.8 Needs of the Bar and Subordinate Judiciary are not met by the graduates from the existing 700 and odd law schools:

3.8.1 Recently,.the Supreme Court of India has observed in **All India Judges Association vs. Union of India** (2002) 3 SCALE 291 = (2002) 4 SCC 247, (2002) 2 SCR 712 = AIR 2002 SC 1752 that recruitment rules in the States should be amended to permit raw graduates from the law schools to enter the subordinate judiciary. Obviously, this requires a high degree of proficiency from the students who pass from the law schools. It should be our objective to improve the standards of all the law schools to the standards required in the present age. Otherwise, the quality of the bar and the subordinate judiciary is bound to go down further. There is, in fact, an urgent need for a fresh probe into the quality of legal education in several law schools and if it is revealed that the standards are poor, it may be necessary to direct closure of such law schools.

3.8.2 Further, it has been noticed that in the last fifteen years, ever since the NLSUs have been established, meritorious students both from NLSUs and some other law schools are joining law firms and corporate houses in greater numbers than those who opt for the bar and the subordinate judiciary. One of the objects of establishing the NLSUs was to improve the quality of the bar and the subordinate judiciary. While it cannot be disputed that such brilliant students are necessary for leading law firms and corporate houses to meet the challenges of globalization, we should not forget that unless these students are attracted to the bar, subordinate judiciary and academia, the quality of legal services cannot be improved.

3.8.3 Senior Counsel in the Trial Courts, High Courts and the Supreme Court must be generous in attracting this talent by offering them good compensation so that all of them may not get attracted to the law firms and corporate houses. As the pay scales of Junior Civil Judges have been enhanced after the implementation of the recommendations of the Jagannatha Shetty Commission, some of these students, if they join the subordinate judiciary at a young age, there are good chances of their reaching the High Court.

3.9 Bar Council of India ought to have taken steps to have legislation passed for reintroduction of the bar examination:

3.9.1 As in all countries, in India too, a bar examination had to be passed whenever law graduates sought enrolment as lawyers. Such an examination was being conducted by the State Bar Councils under the provisions of the Advocates Act, 1961 but the provision relating to bar examination was deleted by amendment of the statute in 1973. However, after the Ahmadi Committee Report (1994) recommended reintroduction of the bar examination, the requirement was reintroduced by a way of a Rule made by the Bar Council of India. The Supreme Court, in: 1999 (3) SCC 176 declared the Rule as *ultra vires* as **Sudheer vs. Bar Council of India** such a requirement has to be introduced only by amending the Advocates Act, 1961. The Supreme Court went further and made a clear recommendation that the requirement of bar examination must be reintroduced into the Act by a statutory amendment. Unfortunately, the BCI which is to take care of standards for purpose of entry into the bar has not taken steps to have the Act amended by reintroduction of the bar examination, in spite of the observations of the Supreme Court in **Sudheer** and in spite of the specific recommendation of the Law Commission in its 184th Report (2002) (Para 12.16).

3.9.2 From the above discussion, it is clear that the present quality of most of the 700 and odd law schools does not meet the domestic needs of our trade and commerce nor the needs for the purposes of recruitment to the subordinate judiciary. This quality should be improved by taking various steps such as bringing in better faculty and, better libraries. As stated above, the law schools must be compelled to offer a large number of optional subjects to meet the needs of the present times.

3.10 Challenge of delivering justice to the poor:

3.10.1 The main challenge facing India's legal and judicial systems is delivering justice to poor people. For the most part, people deprived of Constitutional or legislative rights have little access to courts. With the cost of good quality legal services escalating, the ability of common people to get effective, high quality legal assistance and access to justice is diminishing and the legal system is in danger of becoming further alienated from common people. New and innovative solutions are needed to ensure that common people have access to justice and that legal ideas and legal knowledge protect their interest. Increasing numbers of the best law graduates are moving to corporate law practice and civil and criminal litigation at the local level is suffering from a serious dearth of adequately qualified legal professionals. It is, therefore, imperative that legal education should prepare students with the aptitude, interest, commitment, skills and knowledge necessary to work with socially excluded people and the poor at the local level, to advance the cause of justice.

3.11 Domestic needs and needs of Globalization: Need for a new 'Regulator' with a global vision:

3.11.1 We next come to the crucial issue of the needs of globalization. The Law Commission in its 184th Report, (2002) (Para 5.16) has pointed out that there are revolutionary changes which have come into legal education by reason of developments in information, communication, transport technologies, intellectual property, corporate law, cyber law, human rights, ADR, international business, comparative taxation laws, space laws, environmental laws, etc. and that:

"The very nature of law, legal institutions and law practice are in the midst of a paradigm shift".

3.11.2 The aim of transnational legal education is not to create individuals who can 'practice' law in a number of jurisdictions. Although graduates of such a programme may well wish to do so, such ability should not be seen as an objective in itself, but merely as an incidental result. The aim of any new programme should be to create lawyers who are comfortable and skilled in 'dealing' with the differing legal systems and cultures that make up our global community while remaining strong in one's own national legal system. Our lawyers must be trained to specialize in international trade practices, comparative law, conflict of laws, international human rights law, environmental law, gender justice, space law, biomedical law, bioethics, international advocacy etc., They must also acquire a general knowledge of American, French, German, Chinese and Japanese law. For example, in South Korea, in the last 10 years, the curriculum has been expanded to include not only the above subjects, but also International Business, International Contracts, International Civil Procedure and laws of England, America, France and Germany.

3.11.3 Globalization does not merely mean addition or inclusion of new subjects in the curriculum as stated above. While that is, no doubt, an important matter, the broader issue is to prepare the legal profession to handle the challenges of globalization. Prof. David E Van Zandt of North-West University School of Law states in his article 'Globalization Strategies for Legal Education' (2002, Vol. 34, *University of Toledo Law Review)* as follows:

"Any law dean worth his or her salt will tell alumni and students that it is important for their school to be 'international''.

As businesses become more global, CEOs increasingly bring in savvy general counsel who find and manage firms and lawyers who will do a great job no matter where in the world they are located. Businesses look for service providers whose practices are in line with the company's philosophy, regardless of nationality. We thus see a set of international conventions emerging with respect to the legal structuring of transactions and dispute resolution. The legal practices in capital market transactions have long been largely homogenized around the world, given the pressure of highly mobile capital.

In terms of legal services, these changes have developed a standard set of practices that lawyers use in dealing with the needs of significant business clients whose operations have international scope. Whether a lawyer is working for multinational clients in Hongkong, Frankfurt, London, Buenos Aires, or New York, the set of practices is largely the same. This enables a skilled lawyer to move effortlessly around the world.

This obviously goes far beyond preparing graduates only for practice at the bar or for the subordinate judiciary.

3.12 Steps which have to be taken to prepare legal education to meet various challenges, in addition to changes in curriculum:

3.12.1 Apart from expanding the curriculum, law schools have to improve their libraries; the students and faculty must be able to draw regularly from the internet. Use of computers and internet must be made compulsory in all law schools. So far as the faculty is concerned, experience in other countries shows that video-conferencing of lectures by foreign faculty can help in overcoming the shortage of teachers having knowledge of new subjects. The next thing that is being done elsewhere is the exchange of faculty for short periods, wherever finances permit.

3.12.2 Legal education must be socially engaged. This means that legal education programmes must compulsorily expose students to the problems of poverty, social exclusion, social change and environmental degradation through clinical legal education, legal aid programmes and through seminars and debates that sensitize and expose students to issues of social justice. Working with the poor through one or other programme must become a mandatory part of the curriculum. Faculty must include individuals with interdisciplinary training and direct experience on social issues.

3.12.3 In some countries, law schools are tying up or partnering with foreign law schools. For this purpose, an alliance of law schools has to be brought into being so that the domestic as well as the foreign law schools may mutually benefit and, in such alliances, the cost is to be shared. The syllabi can be changed to have a common core of transnational curriculum. Block teaching allocations are also now common under which, both students and faculty listen directly to foreign faculty or to lectures by video-conferencing. Today, collaboration with foreign universities is resulting, in some countries, in award of two degrees simultaneously. (See the series of Articles by eminent Professors in Vol. 55 (2004) of the *Journal of Legal Education*, pp. 475 to 541.)

3.12.4 Prof. Van Zandt emphasizes the need for an international faculty, international courses, exchange opportunities, international student infusion and summer-abroad programmes so as to prepare students for global practice. He laments the conservatism of law schools in not moving into international dimensions due to lawyer regulation of legal education. He says:

"Despite these changes, law schools throughout the world have remained very traditional. These features of lawyer regulation and education have combined to reduce innovation and create artificial shortages of lawyers, which in turn reduces the pressure from market forces......"

3.12.5 That exactly summarizes the position in India created by the existing regulator. While Indian industry and businesses have expanded beyond national boundaries into other continents and while international business investments into India have come to stay, the bulk of our law schools operate in isolation and focus only on local needs and not even upon the needs of the nation, let alone regional or international needs. This situation that has been created can be broken only by establishing an independent regulatory mechanism with an international vision, which can see beyond the requirements of 'entry into the bar'.

3.13 A new regulatory mechanism is needed with powers to deal with all aspects of legal education:

3.13.1 In the light of the changed scenario in the last fifty years, the needs of globalization after 1991, and the gaps and deficiencies in the existing system as referred to above which have to be filled up, it is clear that the BCl has neither the power under the Advocates Act, 1961 nor the expertise to meet the new challenges both domestically and internationally. It is, therefore, necessary to constitute a new regulatory mechanism with a vision both of social and international goals, to deal with all aspects of legal education and to cater to the needs of the present and the future. Such a mechanism will have to be vested with powers to deal with all aspects of legal education. However, the recommendations of the BCI in regard to maintenance of minimum standards for the purpose of 'practice in courts' will have to be binding on the new Regulator. The directives of the new Regulatory Mechanism must be treated as binding on the law schools, the Universities and on the Union and State Governments. The new regulator has to prevent dilution of the minimum standards by any of the players. For example, it has been reported recently that in some States, the Governments have passed orders reducing the minimum marks to be obtained at the common entrance examination for law to 35% or even below 35% in some cases, only with a view to enable all law schools in that State, most of which are substandard, to fill up all the remaining unfilled seats!

3.13.2 As stated at the outset, in the Report of the National Knowledge Commission 2006 released recently the proposal is to have an Independent Regulatory Authority for Higher Education (IRAHE) with several Standing Committees including one for legal education (vide page 55). It is also proposed that the following Acts namely those relating to UGC, All-India Council for Technical Education ("AICTE"), MCI and BCI will have to be amended.

We, accordingly, propose the setting up of a Standing Committee on Legal Education whose recommendations will be taken into account by the new regulator, the IRAHE. The new Standing Committee on Legal Education may consist of a group of persons including eminent lawyers, members of the Bar Council of India, judges, jurists, academicians, eminent men from trade, commerce and industry, economists, eminent social workers, student representatives and others so that legal education can be revamped to meet the needs and challenges of all sections of society in the next five decades.

3.13.3 It is suggested that the new Standing Committee on Legal Education may consist of 25 members as follows:

(a) One will be a retired judge of the Supreme Court and preferably the retired judge of the Supreme Court who is the Chairman of the Legal Education Committee of the Bar Council of India;

(b) Seven members from the legal profession of which five will be nominated by the Bar Council of India and two will be nominated by the IRAHE;

(c) Seven from the faculty;

(d) One from the government;

(e) Two to be nominated from the industry, trade and commerce;

(f) One from civil society;

(g) Two from other professions;

(h) One from management or other institutions having a legal component;

(i) One parliamentarian; and

(j) Two students of the final year, one representing the NLSUs and the other representing the other law schools (Non-voting representation).

All the members, except the five lawyers to be nominated by the Bar Council of India, have to be nominated by the IRAHE.

3.13.4 The BCI will continue to exercise its powers to recommend the minimum standards required for practice in the courts and such recommendations shall be binding on the IRAHE. Of course, the Bar Council of India will continue to enjoy its powers of discipline so far as the members of the bar are concerned.

3.13.5 The Standing Committee on Legal Education shall have authority to recommend to the IRAHE on the following matters:

(a) Laying down broad standards of legal education in all its aspects including standards for practice in the courts, provided that it shall enforce the minimum standards recommended by the Bar Council of India for the purpose of practice in the courts;

(b) Laying down conditions for admission of students and conduct of entrance examinations in each State and laying down the procedures of counseling and allocation of students to various law schools;

(c) Prescribing the curriculum, the syllabus, the number of compulsory and optional subjects and taking steps to provide for research;

(d) Qualifications and experience of law teachers and number of teaching hours;

(e) Establishment of training institutes for law teachers;

(f) Conditions for affiliation and recognition of law schools by the universities;

(g) Attendance requirements for students;

(h) Inspection of law schools and their accreditation;

(i) Ensuring autonomy for law schools so far as the optional subjects are concerned and prescribing regulations to prevent dilution of standards;

(j) Taking steps to improve the quality of legal education in all law schools to the standards of the NLSUs and to meet the challenges of the domestic needs and the needs of globalization.

As already stated, the recommendations of the Standing Committee on Legal Education shall be considered by the IRAHE. The recommendations of the Bar Council of India under the Advocates Act, 1961 shall, however, be binding on the IRAHE insofar as they relate to minimum standards of legal education required for purposes of entry into the Bar.

CHAPTER IV

CENTRES FOR ADVANCED LEGAL STUDIES AND RESEARCH (CALSAR)

4.1 In the era of globalization, the production of ideas has assumed a critical role — both for social justice and for economic and technological advancement. If India has to fulfill its promise of becoming a global power, it is crucial that we invest in knowledge production and the dissemination as well as make provision for adequate research to address the range of issues and questions involved. This is as true in the domain of law. The ongoing liberalization process raises complex issues relating to the nature of legal reforms necessary to ensure the development of all sections of the population. The growing harmonization of legal rules at the international level in different areas of economic and social life also poses its own challenges of determining our national interests. The need to understand other legal traditions and cultures also require attention.

4.2 There is, therefore, an urgent need to set up four centres for advanced legal studies and research (CALSAR), one in each region. Such regional centres may be established using a base model with the mandate for promoting legal studies and research, and shall enjoy full autonomy. Some of the tasks to be assigned to these advanced legal centres would include cutting-edge research on developing subjects and related areas, as well as serve as a think-tank for advising the government in national and international fora. Some of the specific functions and objectives of these centres would include the following:

- Bringing out a peer reviewed journal of international quality;
- Encouraging interaction across disciplines to facilitate a multidisciplinary approach to understanding law;
- Institutionalizing arrangements for having national and international scholars in residence;
- Organizing workshops and conferences on contemporary developments and issues of law;
- Undertaking in-depth research projects on new and developing areas of law, including specializing in some branches of law;
- Providing continuing legal education for faculty members of law schools. All faculty members would be required to attend and clear minimum number of courses for promotion to professor grade;

- Courses/research subjects to include pedagogy, university management and administration, use of technology in legal education, etc.
- Building a world-class library, with up-to-date and easily accessible resources, including online resources and a national network;
- Establishing a network with other international law research institutions to exchange information and access resources worldwide;

4.3 Each CALSAR would require an initial investment of around ₹ 50 crore (necessary for building anacademic complex, conferencing facilities, library and other infrastructure). These institutes would also be provided with an annual budget to the tune of ₹ 5 crore (for salaries, fellowships, administrative expenses, etc). The infrastructure should be of international standards. This initial investment and the annual budgets should be borne by the Central and respective State governments (that will host the CALSAR) respectively, but it should be financially self-sustaining.

Self-sustenance could be achieved in the following ways:

- Nominal fees could be charged for faculty training that could be levied on the faculty member's institution alone or could be shared with the faculty member.
- Paid training programmes for the industry/profession to be conducted on the lines of executive training programmes for business managers. The programmes shall also be open for faculty members to ensure that training relevant for the industry is delivered to the academia as well.
- Lectures delivered to be recorded and sold in India and abroad.
- Government may tie-up with universities abroad for lectures to be transmitted to these universities through video-conferencing for a price. These lectures may also be exchanged for lectures by faculty of leading universities.

4.4 Foreign scholars may be invited to these institutes for short-term stays (from a semester to a year) to create a stimulating environment for serious research. These institutions would need to be provided with appropriate academic infrastructure that matches the best in the world (e.g., Max Planck Institutes in Germany).

CHAPTER V

ACCESS, ATTRACTING, RETAINING TALENTED FACULTY AND FINANCING OF LEGAL EDUCATION

5.1 Access

5.1.1 While the immediate task may be to improve the quality of legal education, the question of access is an equally serious one. There is need to simultaneously address quality and access issues. There are three kinds of issues that need to be addressed here. *First,* there is the need for more law schools to meet the demands of an expanding legal services market. *Second,* there is the need to ensure the ready availability of loans and scholarships for needy students. *Third,* there are issues of access to a range of academic activities, such as mooting and participating in conferences that require financial support. Several law schools have successfully made arrangements with leading banks to facilitate the availability of loans to needy students. This practice can be emulated by other law schools. The legal community, especially members of the bar, should be requested to support a wide range of academic programmes and activities in law schools.

5.2 Explore methods of attracting and retaining talented faculty members

5.2.1 In order to attract and retain talented faculty members, there is an urgent need to improve their remuneration and service conditions. *First,* the current UGC scales offered by the law schools and universities are not sufficiently attractive. *Second,* the teaching load needs to be rationalized in order to leave sufficient time for research purposes. *Third,* there is need to institute both at national and institutional levels, awards to honor reputed law teachers and researchers. *Fourth,* there has to be sufficient flexibility with law schools to appoint law teachers without having an LL.M. degree if the individual has proven academic or professional credentials. *Fifth,* there is a need to reconsider the existing promotional schemes and avenues in order to promote meritorious faculty members. Incentives such as fully paid sabbaticals should also be granted. *Sixth,* free faculty housing is another significant incentive that may be considered.

5.2.2 Faculty exchange programmes with leading universities abroad would help in enriching the knowledge base and familiarizing faculty members with other legal systems and innovative pedagogic methods.

5.2.3 Video-conferencing of lectures by foreign faculty can help in overcoming the shortage of teachers with knowledge of new subjects. The next thing that is being done elsewhere is the exchange of faculty for short periods, wherever finances permit.

5.2.4 Young faculty members may be permitted to be associated with courts or law firms or corporate houses for brief periods of time in order to acquire practical knowledge. Appropriate infrastructure facilities to faculty, including the availability of computers, internet and access to online journals and legal databases may be considered.

5.3 Financing legal education

5.3.1 It is estimated that a law school needs a minimum annual budget of ₹ 5 crore to ensure adequate number of faculty members, a proper administrative staff, infrastructure facilities including a well endowed library, computer facilities, quality teaching materials, conference facilities, guest houses, etc. are available.

5.3.2 It is felt that it is the responsibility of the State for making adequate financial provisions. Unless the State finances legal education, it is difficult to ensure access to quality legal education at affordable costs. The alternative would be to evolve appropriate public private partnerships to finance legal education. Central and state ministries may also be urged to endow chairs on specialized branches of law. Such financing can be complemented with endowments from the private sector.

5.3.3 The latest innovation is acquisition of joint degrees by a student namely the degree of his own university as well as the degree of a foreign university with which there is a partnership during the same period. For example, in Puerto Rico (Caribbean), in the last few years, dual degree programmes have been started in conjunction with certain universities in Barcelona (Spain) and Minnesota (USA). To these graduates, the opportunities are unlimited. If we adopt such a system, the businesses and markets of our country can greatly benefit from the knowledge of such graduates.

5.3.4 Institutions must find ways to maximize infrastructure and resource utilization, such as, addition of more students, running separate morning and evening batches, and having spring and fall terms like in the US.

5.3.5 Infrastructure sharing — It is felt that there must be co-ordination between institutions for the purposes of sharing of infrastructure.

Institutions with existing libraries, sport facilities, etc. can share these facilities with other institutions for a fixed fee. New institutions can develop facilities in such manner that facilitate sharing, for instance, an institution having more land may invest in sports facilities while the other may develop an excellent library.

5.3.6 Commercialize infrastructure — Libraries may be opened to public access. Sports facilities, conference halls, etc. may be opened for public use at such time when they are not in use, for instance, in the evenings or during vacations.

5.3.7 Lectures delivered by good faculty can be recorded and sold in India and abroad.

5.3.8 Tax holidays — Donations above a high minimum threshold to educational institutions by corporates could be granted tax exemption up to three-fourths of sum donated. Companies would be keen to associate their names to educational projects while availing tax benefits. In return, it shall build the much-required initial point of contact between institutions and corporates that can be developed for further benefits. It shall also ensure that money percolates straight to the institutions rather than flowing from the tax-payer to the government to the institution, and being wasted in the process.

5.3.9 The Working Group on legal education consisted of the following members:

1. Justice M. Jagannadha Rao (Chairperson)
2. Justice Leila Seth
3. Dr. Madhav Menon
4. Mr. P.P. Rao
5. Dr. B.S. Chimni
6. Mr. Nishith Desai
7. Dr. Mohan Gopal

As Chairperson and on behalf of all members of the said Working Group, I hereinunder sign and deliver this report on legal education for the consideration of the National Knowledge Commission.

Regards,

Sincerely,

(Justice M. Jagannadha Rao)

March 5, 2007

CHAPTER VIII
ROAD MAP AHEAD

Will, let me suggest some immediate steps to be taken in the educational/ training sector which are necessary in the shaping of a world-class legal system as described above.

1. Distinguish professional legal education from the rest and identify professional law schools to be given autonomy and infrastructural support towards giving them a fair chance to show competitive excellence of world quality.

2. Divest Bar Council of India of its legal education regulation function and vest it on an independent Regulator, the Higher Education commission, as recommended by the National Knowledge Commission and the Yashpal Committee.

3. Reintroduce compulsory apprenticeship and pre-admission professional entrance examination for all those seeking entry to the Bar. Make continuing education in selected law schools on a prescribed curriculum mandatory for all advocates every five years.

4. Establish independent Mediation and Arbitration Councils on the model of the Bar Council and initiate separate licensing system with disciplinary bodies for mediators and arbitrators.

5. Develop an all-India prosecutorial service and specialized training programmes for at least one year to all prosecutors. Institute rigorous performance standards and weed out those who are inefficient or corrupt. Reward performance of Prosecutors through promotions even to the judiciary.

6. Establish an all·India Judicial Service and impart specialized training for at least on year on a prescribed curriculum. Performance assessment should be on objective criteria and transparent process. Fast track promotion be introduced to reward merit and hard work.

7. Reorganize legal aid services under an independent corporation with equal participation of lawyers, judges and consumers of justice (NGOs).

8. Establish few Advanced Legal Research Centres wit specific mandate for policy development, legislative drafting, judicial impact assessment, proposals for institutional reform and criteria for performance assessment of legal and judicial institutions/personnel.

9. Create a managerial cadre of duly qualified and well-trained personnel to manage the judiciary at all levels. Create a database on judicial statistics and make judicial planning and budgeting evidence-based.

10. Establish a department of Criminal Justice at Central and State levels under a high-powered board representing judiciary, police, prosecution and Home accountable to Parliament/Assembly as the case may be. Let the Forensic Science Laboratories work directly under this Board to be chaired by a Supreme Court/High Court judge.

BIBLIOGRAPHY AND REFERENCES

1. Bhagwati Prasad Srivastava, "The Role of Lawyer in the Changing Society", Golden Jubilee Commomoration, Dec. 26, 1982, p-85.

2. N.C. Gupta, "Evolution of Ancient India Law", p.41.

3. Justice Deoki Nandan, High Court, Allhabad, "Role of Lawyers in Democratic Body Politic", Golden Jubilee Commomoration, Dec. 26, 1982, pp. 17-18. See also Prof. M.L. Upadhayay, "The Bar Council in India: Prospect and Retrospect", at p.37; Sri Banwari Lal Yadav, The Bar Council and the Noble Profession of Law, p.49.

4. Sushma Gupta, History of Legal Education, 2004.

5. *Supra,* n.2.

6. See Ludo Rocher, "Lawyers in Classical Hindu Law", IBR, Vol. XII (3 and 4), 1986.

7. B.M. Gandhi and V.D. Kulshrehtha's Landmarks in India — Legal and Constitution History, Sixth edition (1989), p. 450.

   Justice during this period was administered by the company's servants, who had no legal knowledge. Though there were few attornies and solicitors and solicitors to plead before the court (Mayor Court) but they were neither men of character and integrity nor had much legal knowledge. M.P. Jain, Indian Legal History, (1972), p.23.

8. See *Supra,* n.6, p.451. Also, n.7. pp. 622, 623.

   The Bengal Regulation XII of 1833; The Legal Practioners Act, 1846, 1863; The Indian High Courts Act, 1861; The legal Practioners Act, 1879; The Indian Bar Council Act, 1926 were enacted with a view to establish a enlightened Bar which will assist the government in administration of justice in the country.

9. See – Preamble to the Constitution of India; and Art 38(1).

10. S.P. Sathe, "Legal Profession – Its Contribution to Social Change: A Survey of the Pune City Bar, 18 & 19 Ban. L.J. (1982-83), p. 40

11. V.R. Krishna Iyer, "Accountability of Professions," Indian Bar Review, Vol. XIV (4) 1987, p.650 at 655.

12. Draft Universal Declaration on the Independence of Justice, Indian Bar Review, Vol. XIV (4), 1987, p.595 at 603.

13. Independence of Justice, Indian Bar Review. Vol XIV (4), 1987, p.505 at 565.

14. Justice P.K. Tare, "Indian Judicial System and Indian Judiciary", 1993 (VI) CILQ, p. 385 at 386. The learned author remarks that "In High Courts, lawyers demand

fees in four figures in criminal cases, while in the Supreme Court leading Lawyers do not talk except in five figures".

15. N.R. Madhave Menon, "Reforming Legal Education: Issues, Priorities and Proposals", 1979, ISLJ, Vol. V, No. 1 & 2, p.22 at 26.

16. P.K. Tripathi, "In the Quest for Better Legal Education", JILM (1968) Vol. 10, No. 3.

17. See – Justice Gulab Gupta, "Legal Education the Perception of Social Needs and Formulation of Responses", 1989 (I), CILQ, pp. 15-38.

18. *Supra,* n. at p. 563.

19. See – S.K. Agarwala, "Profile of the Indian Law Teacher" (1979), ISLJ, p.1. Foot note 9 at p.3. "A few law colleges only are run by some of the state governments, e.g., Govt. Law College, Bombay; on at Bangalore, on at Madras, 3 in Kerala. Some universities also run thie law colleges but not as university departments, e.g., Nagpur, Waltair (A.P.), about 8 in Madhya Pradesh, Gauhati, Dharwar, Pondicherry, Osmania, Tirupati, Calcutta. The conditions therein are generally somewhere in between those of the university departments and affiliated college.

20. *Supra,* n. 18 at p.6.

21. S.S. Kulshresth, "Legal Education in Madhya Pradesh", 2 GMLJ, 1988-89, p.157 at 164.

22. For number of part-time and full-time teachers in Madhya Pradesh. See *Supra* n. 23 at 159.

23. *Ibid.,* p. 157

24. *Supra* n. 16 at 24, 'According to a sample student in one of the well-known law faculties in a premier university in the country hardly ten per cent of law students join the college with the intention of joining the profession. The rest ninety per cent have landed up on law for a variety of reasons including avoidance of an employment prospect, improvement in job opportunities desire to continue the student status for personal and political reasons, pursuation by parents and friends, inability to get admitted in other professional courses etc. (Delhi Law Review 1971).

25. Dr. S. R. Mvncni, World Trade Organization (WTO), Asia Law House, 2nd edition, 2003.

26. Dr. J.N. Pandey, Constitutional Law of India, Central Law Agency, 44th edition, 2007.

27. Dr. Justice A.S. Anand; H. L. Sarin, Memorial lecture, " Legal Education in India — Past, Present and Future".

28. C. Rajkumar, "Legal Education and Global Philanthropy".

29. C. Rajkumar. "Globalization and Legal Education".

30. General Agreement on Trade in Services (GATS) of WTO.

31. Dr. N.R. Madhava Menon, " Reforming the Legal Profession: Some Ideas".
32. Report of the Working Group on Legal Fducation of The National Knowledge Commission.
33. Justice A.M. Ahmadi, " Reparing the Cracks in Legal Education".
34. C. Rajkumar, "Improving Legal Education in India".
35. *THE HINDU.*
36. www.knovvledgeeommission.gov.in
37. AIR 1973, S.C., 1461.
38. AIR 1996, S.C., L
38. *India Business Law Journal,* May 2003.
39. Report of National Knowledge Commission (2008).

Courtesy: articles by -

1. Mr. Lahotti, R.C. (Justice)
2. Mr. Madhava Menon, N. R. (Prof.)
3. Mr. Puri, K. K. (Prof.)
4. Mr. Sorabjee, Soli J. (Former Attorney General of India)
5. Mr. Tulpule, R. D. (Retd. Justice)
6. Mr. K.N. Chandrasekharan Pillai (Prof.)
7. Dr. Ram Babu Dubey (Prof.)
8. http://en.wikipedia.org/wiki/Autonomous_law_schools_in_India
9. http://news.indlaw.com/guest/education/law/aboutprofession.asp